Days to Remember

Geoffrey Trease

Days to Remember

A GARLAND OF HISTORIC ANNIVERSARIES

Illustrated by Joanna Troughton

HEINEMANN:LONDON

William Heinemann Ltd

15 Queen St, Mayfair, London W1X 8BE

LONDON   MELBOURNE   TORONTO
JOHANNESBURG   AUCKLAND

First published 1973
© Geoffrey Trease 1973
Illustrations © William Heinemann Ltd 1973

434 96762 9

Printed Offset Litho in Great Britain by
Cox & Wyman Ltd, London, Fakenham and
Reading

Contents

AUTHOR'S NOTE

What is special about anniversaries? Most of us, from children with birthdays to whole nations celebrating heroes and victories, find it natural to recall the past event when the exact date comes round again. So I have gathered here, month by month through the calendar, a very personal choice of stories and characters from history that seem to be worth remembering. I have aimed at variety. The items are not all state occasions or gory battles. I have sought out the comic as well as the tragic. I have included many famous persons and familiar episodes, but I was determined also to find a place for some of history's forgotten 'men-in-the-street', whose names have survived only in some obscure archive. In most cases, if the reader wants to learn more than there is space to tell here, he can satisfy his curiosity with whole volumes or at least with a good encyclopaedia.

Geoffrey Trease

January

The Lone Thorn Tree

When the wintry dawn broke on 8 January 871, it showed a lone, leafless thorn tree standing high on the bare chalk downs of Berkshire. It had stood there ever since men could remember. It had become a useful boundary mark, and two centuries later it was to figure in William the Conqueror's Domesday survey as 'Nachededorn', the Naked Thorn.

It was the place King Ethelred of Wessex chose to do battle with the two Danish kings, Bagsac and Halfden, whose invading horde had swept up the Thames Valley as far as Reading, and now threatened to overrun the rest of southern England.

On the previous night the two armies had pitched camp on opposite slopes, with the thorn tree between them in no man's land and the prehistoric ridgeway track running pale white in the darkness from one cluster of watch-fires to the other.

When daylight came, Ethelred could see the Danes mustering in two masses to right and left of the trackway. Their banners indicated that the kings were jointly leading one division while their principal 'jarls' or earls headed the other. Ethelred called a council of war and decided that he would similarly divide the Saxon army, himself commanding the half that faced the Danish kings, and giving the other half to his younger brother.

Then, being a devout Christian, he went to hear mass in his tent.

He was quite confident that the enemy would not attack first. They never did. Fierce though the Danes were, and brave beyond question, they did not look for trouble but for loot. They fought only when compelled to. Then it was their habit to take up their stand in a good position and let their enemy come to them.

It had been like that last time, when the Danes had driven him back with heavy losses. They had no reason to change their tactics. But this time Ethelred had gathered strong reinforcements and he believed that, with God's help, the battle would go the other way.

So he knelt before the portable altar in his tent and gave all his mind to the service.

The sacred ceremony was reaching its most solemn moment when, to the horror of the Saxons mustering on the grassy hill, there came a strident blowing of war-horns from the Danish camp and they saw the two masses of gleaming helmets and rippling mail begin to move down the opposite hill towards them.

Little more than half a mile separated the two armies. There was no time to run to the King's tent, burst in upon the service, and ask for orders.

His younger brother knew that in this crisis he must make the decision.

That brother's name was Alfred, a name destined to be famous but at that time little known. He was about twenty-one, delicate in health, and with only that one recent experience – anything but successful – of a full-scale battle against the Danes.

But he knew that he could not just stand there. In a hand-to-hand clash his own side must have the same advantage as their adversaries – the impetus of running full-tilt at the moment of impact.

He gave the signal. Both sections of the army, the King's as well as his own, charged down the slope to meet the enemy.

The bloodiest fighting raged round the lone thorn tree. Young Alfred, men said in later years, was 'like a wild boar'. One of the Danish kings fell, five of the greatest jarls, hundreds of their warriors. The others fled. Alfred, now joined by his elder brother, chased them across the downs to their fortified camp at Reading.

Such was the fight at Ashdown, first in what came to be

known as 'the year of battles', for there were nine in all. A few months afterwards King Ethelred died, and, because his two sons were far too young to lead the people in such a period of crisis, Alfred was elected king by the witan, or council, 'with the full consent of all the inhabitants of the realm'. It was a fortunate choice for England.

Modern experts argue about the exact site of the battle but it was probably in the dip (which gipsies still call Awful Bottom) between Lowbury Hill and Louse Hill, two or three miles from Streatley. There is no lone thorn tree now where the ancient trackways cross – there is a whole cluster of them, surely the descendants of Alfred's tree just as much as we are the children of the Saxons and Danes who fought there?

The Treacle-moon

'The treacle-moon is over, and I am awake, and find myself married.'

Thus, with his usual irony and scorn for sentiment, Lord Byron wrote to his Irish friend and fellow-poet, Thomas Moore, at the end of a honeymoon which had been singularly devoid of romance.

The ill-fated wedding had taken place on 2 January 1815 – and Waterloo was not the only fierce battle that was to be fought in that historic year.

Byron was twenty-seven. To be exact, his birthday fell during 'the treacle-moon' on 22 January.

For the past three years his poetry had been a main topic of conversation in England and even in Europe. After the publication of *Childe Harold's Pilgrimage*, 'I awoke one morning,' Byron confessed, 'and found myself famous.'

It is hard today to imagine the sensational effect that his poems produced. They were long works, full of colour and passion, and – except that they were in ringing verse – they were more equivalent to a modern romantic best-selling novel, with an element of the popular travel-book as well. *Childe Harold's Pilgrimage* ran through seven editions in four weeks.

Not only was Byron the best-selling author of the day, but he was young, strikingly if rather devilishly handsome, and a nobleman into the bargain – in a period when to be a lord meant infinitely more than it does now.

Above all, he was unmarried. His charm was irresistible –

and the married women in the fashionable drawing-rooms of London could no more resist it than could the girls.

One was Lady Caroline Lamb, whose life was wrecked by her hopeless passion for him. 'Bad, mad and dangerous to know,' was her oft-quoted verdict on Byron.

His final choice of a woman to marry was one of the many strange things in an extraordinary life.

Annabella Milbanke was a quiet, serious young woman from the north of England, utterly different from the girls who flocked round him in the great London houses. She studied mathematics, philosophy and classical literature in an age when few women were given the chance to study anything at all, let alone the first two subjects. Jokingly Byron called her 'the amiable Mathematician' and his 'Princess of Parallelograms'. Yet she intrigued him, and up to a point attracted him.

There was another attraction. Though at present she had no money she would one day inherit a fortune. Byron himself was always desperate for money. He had lavish tastes, far beyond his means, and a foolish pride – he cared far more for his dignity as a peer than for his glory as a poet – prevented him from accepting the money earned by his books.

So primarily Byron was driven to court Annabella for the sake of her future fortune. She, for her part, accepted him in the pathetic hope that she could reform his scandalous way of life and bring out the basic goodness in his nature. They became engaged in September 1814, both impelled by the wrong reasons, neither passionately in love with the other.

There were no elaborate preparations for the wedding – except perhaps by the lawyers of both families who had to draw up complicated 'settlements' to cover the financial arrangements, present and future. The ceremony itself was to be private, by licence, at the home of the bride in County Durham. It was a quite common occurrence at that time, and the avoidance of a 'grand' wedding suited everybody, not least the girl's father, who was heavily in debt.

They planned the marriage for mid-December, but Byron

decided that he wanted to spend Christmas with his half-sister, Augusta, for whom he seems to have felt a far more passionate love than for his betrothed. After Christmas he drove north with one close friend, John Cam Hobhouse, and at last, on 2 January, kneeling on a hard cushion in the drawing-room at Seaham House, he was joined in matrimony with his 'Princess of Parallelograms'.

'We were married yesterday at ten upon the clock,' he wrote to Lady Melbourne. 'So there's an end of that matter, and the beginning of many others . . . All those who are disposed to make presents may as well send them forthwith, and pray let them be handsome.'

Annabella's parents, Sir Ralph and Lady Milbanke, lent them another family residence, Halnaby House, for what Byron was soon to describe as 'the treacle-moon'. After a few weeks they went back to stay with the Milbankes at Seaham House, scene of their unromantic marriage.

Byron suffered agonies of boredom. Not, he insisted in a letter to Lady Melbourne, with his newly-acquired wife – though one cannot help wondering, for it seems odd for a bridegroom even to consider the possibility – but with his father-in-law. Sir Ralph was very pleased with himself because of a political speech he had recently delivered in Durham. He was apt to go over it again when the two men were left to their port after dinner. Once the poet slipped away from the table and began a letter to Moore, describing the tedium of Sir Ralph's interminable oration.

'He is now, I believe, speaking it to himself (I left him in the middle) over various decanters, which can neither interrupt him nor fall asleep – as might possibly have been the case with some of his audience.'

Byron was thankful to get away from that 'dreary' coast and the drearier company. He was hungry for the gaieties of London, where they were to rent a house at – ominous number – 13 Piccadilly Terrace. On the way, he was anxious to visit his married half-sister.

'Take care of Annabella,' his mother-in-law instructed him as she saw them into their coach. And as the horses moved forward, Byron turned to the unfortunate girl and demanded irritably: 'What on earth does your mother mean? I suppose you can take care of yourself.'

Such a marriage was foredoomed to unhappiness. In the following January – on the fifteenth, to be precise – as Byron slept on in his separate room, Annabella tiptoed downstairs and climbed into the carriage waiting outside the house. With the baby girl, Augusta Ada, born to her only five weeks earlier, she drove away to her parents. Now not only was the treacle-moon over, but the whole marriage.

Why, it may be asked, in a world that has seen millions of tragic, broken marriages, is Byron's of any historic interest?

Several reasons can be given.

The resulting scandal destroyed his social position in England and virtually drove him into exile in Italy. It thus profoundly affected the rest of his life and the development of his poetry. Had the marriage never taken place, or had it turned out less disastrously, he might not have died at Missolonghi only nine years later, helping the Greeks in their war of independence against the Turks. And in a more general sense the marriage illustrates an aspect of life in bygone times that is now remote to us – the choice of a wife or a husband not for love but for obvious considerations of money and title.

The Frost Fair

On 9 January 1684, near the end of Charles II's reign, the sober and scholarly Mr John Evelyn went to dine with the Archbishop of Canterbury at his London palace of Lambeth on the south bank of the Thames.

This in itself does not sound very remarkable. What is interesting is that, to get there from Westminster, Evelyn did not as usual take a ferry – there were no bridges then nearer than London Bridge far down-river close to the Tower – but was able to walk straight across without wetting his buckled shoes.

The Thames was frozen hard. It had become a town in itself. Whole streets of temporary shops had been erected and were doing a roaring trade in every kind of goods. Fires were blazing to roast meat. The ice was so thick that carts and coaches could safely drive over. A month later, on 5 February, Evelyn himself drove across in his coach.

It was a gay scene, rather shocking to a man of his quiet tastes and religious views. In his diary he noted the 'sliding with skates, a bull-baiting, horse and coach-races, puppet-plays and interludes, cooks, tippling, and other lewd places, so that it seemed to be a Bacchanalian triumph, or carnival on the water . . .' Most people, however, called it a 'frost fair'.

One enterprising man set up a printing press, and for sixpence a time people could have their names printed on souvenir cards, with the date and the inscription, 'Printed on the river of Thames being frozen'. Evelyn reckoned that the printer was clearing five pounds a day for this idea, apart from the ballads and other items he was selling.

The demand for such souvenirs indicates that the Frost Fair was an unusual event but it was certainly not unique. The Thames froze more easily in those days. It was a shallower, more sluggish river for several reasons. Old London Bridge, with its nineteen arches, served as a partial barrier slowing up the flow of the water. Instead of being kept in a deep narrow channel by embankments, the river was free to spread sideways – the very name of the Strand is a reminder that the Thames once washed over the low ground which now carries roadway, pleasure-gardens and buildings. Modern drainage, too, brings rainwater quickly into the river, whereas in earlier centuries it would percolate far more slowly through the soil. Finally, there is the warmth of waste water discharged from power-stations, factories and even house-hold sinks and bathrooms, affecting the temperature, and the warmer air of a vast city using the heating systems now general.

So Frost Fairs crop up from time to time in bygone centuries. January was the usual month, as in 1608, when Shakespeare was still busy in the London theatre. The Dutch artist, Abraham Hondius, has left a fine oil painting of the people enjoying them-

selves near London Bridge in 1676. And as late as 1814, at the end of the Napoleonic period, the caricaturist George Cruikshank drew a lively scene which shows another enterprising printer doing brisk business, while other people are playing ninepins, playing the fiddle, making up to attractive young women, buying gin and gingerbread, and falling about in all directions on the ice.

That was the last of the great Frost Fairs. There was a cold January in 1820, with five feet of ice on the river and people walking about on it again, but for some reason the usual carnival spirit did not fully develop. Could it have been because the old King George III was dying and passed away at the end of the month? It seems unlikely.

Whatever the reason, Londoners never had another chance to enjoy 'all the fun of the fair' on their frozen river, for a few years later the old London Bridge was demolished, and the new one, with only five arches, did not obstruct the flow of water in the same way. Embankments and other changes followed swiftly throughout the next century, so that, however hard the winter, the Thames would never freeze so deeply again.

Robert Burns – 'The Immortal Memory'

On Burns Night all over the world, wherever a few Scots can be gathered together, the haggis is carried to the table to the skirl of the bagpipes and whisky-glasses are raised to toast 'the Lassies' and 'the immortal memory' of the poet.

Many of those present may not care much for poetry. But they have at least a nodding acquaintance with such favourites as 'Tam o' Shanter', 'My love is like a Red, Red Rose', 'Auld Lang

Syne', 'Scots wha hae', 'To a Mouse' and 'Ye Flowery Banks o' Bonny Doon'.

Burns, too, is honoured not only as a poet and a song-writer but as a national figure. When he was born, on 25 January 1759, Scotland seemed to be losing her sense of individuality. She had given up her own Parliament and accepted the Act of Union with England, she had suffered cruelties and humiliations such as the Massacre of Glencoe and the Jacobite defeat at Culloden, and some of her sons (like James Boswell) were apologetic about the country that had borne them.

Burns (aided by Sir Walter Scott a few years later) did much to change all that and revive the pride in Scottish speech and history.

He was the son of a small farmer at Alloway, near Ayr, in the southwestern lowlands. The family was poor and hard-working, but young Robert got some basic education from the village schoolmaster and from his own father, while from his mother's lips he learned the ballads and folk-tales that were to influence his own compositions so deeply.

He loved words. At meals he sat with a book held in one hand while the other spooned up his broth or porridge. As he drove the plough – and he was a skilled ploughman at fifteen – he was making up poems and reciting them to the empty fields.

At sixteen he wrote his first song, 'Handsome Nell', inspired by a girl working beside him at the harvest. Then began a whole series of love-affairs, which won him a wild reputation. It was not long, too, before he was drinking more than was good for him.

He tried various work without much success. He learned surveying and then the trade of flax-dressing. He considered going out to a book-keeping job in Jamaica. He went back to farming and struggled for four years to make a farm pay in partnership with his brother. When that failed he got a government post as an exciseman, collecting taxes.

Meanwhile, in 1786, when trying to raise his passage-money to Jamaica, he published his first volume, *Poems Chiefly in the Scottish*

Dialect. It brought him a good deal of notice. He was invited to Edinburgh and taken up by some of the nobility and intellectuals there. When he joined his brother in the farming venture, the local gentry treated him with new respect. There was even a suggestion that he should put in for the professorship of agriculture at Edinburgh University, where courses in that subject had just been started, but the notion did not appeal to him. Clearly, though, he was not considered the illiterate ploughman that some people imagine him when they know neither his writings nor the details of his life.

That life was shortened by his heavy drinking. He died on 25 July 1796, only thirty-seven, leaving behind him a wealth of poetry, full of feeling and satirical humour, and in the words of the Burns Night toast an 'immortal memory'.

The Secret Diary

New Year is the favourite time for making good resolutions in general and – in particular – for starting a diary. Samuel Pepys is famous for both. As the year 1659 drew to a close he went to the stationer's and bought himself an octavo notebook. Always neat and methodical, he ruled margins in red ink, and on the first day of 1660, that most eventful year in English history, began what was destined to become a classic read and loved by millions.

That was pure accident. He had no intention that anyone should read it, and he took very considerable pains that they should not. He succeeded so well that it was a century and a half before anyone did.

On that New Year's Day Pepys (whose name was pronounced 'peeps') was twenty-six, a London tailor's son, humbly employed as a government clerk and living in Whitehall. He had great ambitions but little idea how far they would lead him. In fact, he was destined to end his days as one of the most respected men in England. He would sit in Parliament, he would enjoy the friendship of two kings, he would be President of the Royal Society and hobnob with scientific geniuses like Newton, and he would be known as the man who had rescued the Navy from ruin and decay.

But all that lay in the future. And on 1 January 1660, the future seemed obscure and dangerous.

As a child Pepys had lived through the Civil War. As a schoolboy with Roundhead sympathies, like most people in the tradesman class and particularly in the City of London, he had stood in the crowd to see King Charles I beheaded, and had rejoiced in the downfall of the Cavaliers.

Now, however, Oliver Cromwell had been dead for more than a year. His son, Richard, had not the strong personality needed to follow him as Lord Protector. The country was divided and seemed on the brink of revolution, the army generals at loggerheads with the remnant of the old Parliament and many people whispering that it would be best to bring back the dead King's son from exile and proclaim him Charles II.

In such a troubled time it was not safe for a man to be too open with his personal opinions. Pepys wanted to be completely free to set down his most private thoughts, and for this reason he wrote his diary in an early system of shorthand, Shelton's Tachygraphy (or 'swift writing') which he had learnt at Cambridge.

It was not only politics that required caution. Into the diary, over the next nine years, went gossip and grumbles about the men he worked with, notes on his earnings and expenses, and accounts of furtive flirtations with tavern wenches and actresses, as well as the continual rows and reconciliations with his pretty young wife.

The diary was to be for no other eyes, least of all hers. Sometimes, to disguise his secrets still further, Pepys used odd words of Latin, French or Spanish.

When bad eyesight made him give up his diary, nine and a half years later, he had filled six volumes, totalling 3,100 pages and 1,250,000 words. He had given vivid eyewitness accounts of great historical occasions, such as the bringing back of Charles II, the Plague, the Great Fire of London, and the burning of the English fleet by the Dutch. He had left, for students of social history, a rich reservoir of facts about everyday life in his day – taking the reader into the church-pew and the playhouse box, the bookshop, the tavern, the country inn, the Navy Office, the King's palace, the ship's cabin, and almost every imaginable corner of Restoration England. And even for those who were not much interested in history he had left an incomparable human document, the revelation of a lovable if rather roguish personality, a book full of humour which could be read for sheer amusement.

The trouble was that, thanks to the shorthand, no one could read it.

The notebooks, filled with their strange, apparently indecipherable characters that looked like a secret code, were bequeathed with thousands of other books and papers to his old Cambridge college, Magdalene. There they remained in the library, neglected, until 1818, when great public interest was aroused by the publication of another old diary, that of Pepys's friend, John Evelyn. A poor Cambridge student, John Smith, was commissioned to transcribe Pepys's notebooks if he could.

It was a formidable task. It could be seen that the writing was shorthand, but there had been many systems invented, and poor Smith never identified this one as Shelton's, which would have given him the key to the secret. Instead, he had to tackle the job as though it were the cracking of a code. He succeeded. He toiled for three years, receiving a total fee of £200, and a grudging word of thanks in the preface when the *Diary* was published. But his patient digging had uncovered a literary treasure which has only grown more valuable with the passing of time.

February

A Shopkeeper's Night Out

Eighteenth-century life was not all an elegant twirling of fans and snuff-boxes, nor was it all brutality and squalor. The diary of Thomas Turner, who lived from 1729 to 1789, and gave up school-teaching to run a village store in Sussex, contains some lively glimpses of ordinary folk.

On Wednesday, 22 February 1757, the young shopkeeper and his wife set out on foot about four o'clock in the afternoon, bound for a neighbour's house, where they found the local parson and his wife, half a dozen other married couples, and several other people, about twenty in all.

They played 'bragg', a card game rather like poker, until after ten. They then sat down to an ample supper, including four boiled chickens, four boiled ducks, minced veal, sausages, cold roast goose, chicken pasty and ham. There was obviously plenty to wash it down, for afterwards, Mr Turner confesses in his diary, 'our behaviour was far from that of serious, harmless mirth; it was downright obstreperious'. For a former teacher, Mr Turner did not spell impeccably, but he may still have been suffering from a hang-over when he made the entry.

Their diversion, he records, 'was dancing or jumping about . . . singing of foolish healths, and drinking all the time as fast as it could well be poured down; and the parson of the parish was one among the mixed multitude.'

At three o'clock in the morning Mr Turner decided he had drunk enough. Rather ungallantly deserting his wife, he slipped out unnoticed and, though 'very far from sober', was thankful to get safely home 'without even tumbling'. It is a relief to know that Mrs Turner arrived, also without mishap, at ten minutes past five, escorted by their neighbour's servant.

England at this date was locked with France in the Seven Years' War which gave her the foundations of her empire in India and Canada. But clearly not every Englishman – and certainly not Mr Turner – was giving full attention to the momentous historic events taking place outside the village.

The Captive Queen

It was a fair morning for February. The deed to be done was dark enough, but the Dean of Peterborough found comfort in the weather as a sign of God's approval for what had to be done. It 'did, as it were, show favour from Heaven, and commended the justice'.

The scene was the great hall of Fotheringay Castle in Northamptonshire, the date 8 February 1587. A low platform had been set up at one end, as though for a play. There was a single high-backed chair, a black cushion to kneel on, and an ordinary wooden chopping-block, draped like everything else in black velvet.

It had all been done hurriedly. The news, though long awaited, had been brought only yesterday. No one had been sure that Queen Elizabeth would bring herself to sign the death-warrant. She had delayed so long, she was so apt to change her mind. But now, at last, her signature was on the paper. The prisoner had better die at once before Elizabeth changed her mind yet again, and another messenger came galloping from London to countermand the order.

Mary slept little that night. She prayed, she looked back over her life, so soon to end. She had to think of farewell messages and of how to carry herself on that stage the carpenters were hammering together. She had often played a part. She must brace herself for this last performance.

She had never known what it was to be anything but a queen. She was forty-four years old and all those years she had borne the title. She had been Queen of Scots in her cradle. Her father, James V, overwhelmed by the English at the battle of Solway Moss, had heard of her birth as he lay dying.

At six she had been betrothed to the French King's son. Leaving her mother to govern Scotland as Regent, she had gone to France and had been educated there at the court. At fifteen she had married the Dauphin. At seventeen he had succeeded his father. That made her Queen of France as well. But not for long – in the next year, 1560, her young husband had died, making her a widow at eighteen. In 1561 she had gone home to Scotland to take over her own kingdom.

Things had never gone well. Scotland, led by the preacher John Knox, had gone over to the new Protestant religion. Mary, brought up in France, had remained devoutly loyal to the Church of Rome. And in the sixteenth century, all over Europe, Catholics and Protestants were at each other's throats. Wars and rebellions, plots and persecutions, all sprang from the excuse of a difference in religion.

So, between Catholic Mary and the Protestant majority of Scots there had been bitter conflict. Matters had been made worse by Mary's second marriage, to Lord Darnley, and then (after their falling out) by his mysterious murder and her marriage to the principal suspect, Lord Bothwell. Mary's very beauty and charm, with her warm passionate nature, had added to her problems in ruling Scotland.

After seven troubled years the Scottish lords had persuaded her to give up the crown in favour of the little boy she had borne to her second husband. This child became James VI (and later James I of England) and the noblemen saw that he was brought up as a Protestant. After one unsuccessful attempt to win back her crown by armed force, Mary had fled across the border to England and asked for sanctuary from her cousin, Elizabeth I.

That had been nineteen years ago. For nineteen years Mary had travelled from one English castle to another, treated with respect but also as a prisoner. In those nineteen years she had never been allowed to meet her cousin face to face.

It had been a complicated situation. Most of the English were as Protestant as the Scots. And because the Pope had not accepted as lawful the divorce and second marriage of Elizabeth's father, King Henry VIII, Catholics believed that Elizabeth was not lawfully born and could not be the rightful Queen of England.

If she was not, then who? The answer was, her cousin Mary. In God's eyes (they argued) Mary was not merely Queen of Scots and Dowager Queen of France but Queen of England too. Mary herself believed this, and for many of those long tragic years she had dreamed of revolts and rescues and her own restoration to power in the world. In her heart she felt herself three times a queen, but in harsh fact, throughout those nineteen years that were close on half her total life, she was a helpless captive, obeyed only by a handful of her devoted personal staff.

While she lived, she was a constant danger to Elizabeth and the ruling Protestant majority in England. Elizabeth had often wished her dead, but she could not bring herself to arrange her murder. Nor, for a long time, could she bring herself to have Mary put on trial for her secret plotting. If only the Queen of Scots would die naturally of some sickness! If only she had fled to some other country when she left Scotland, and not come to England, saddling Elizabeth with this unwelcome responsibility!

Elizabeth's ministers had nagged her continually. She must think of her subjects and the safety of the realm. Mary's life was that of one woman, and a woman who deserved punishment. Elizabeth must set against *her* life the thousands of innocent lives that might be lost if there was a civil war in England. While Mary lived, there was a constant risk of Spanish invasion.

So a trial had been held in that same hall at Fotheringay. Mary had been found guilty of plotting against Elizabeth. She had been sentenced to death. Then, for several months, Elizabeth had held out against signing the warrant for her execution. At last, petitioned to do so by both Houses of Parliament, after a unanimous vote, she had given way. And now the moment had come.

Mary dressed with care. Knowing that the executioners would have to remove her black velvet gown with the white lace frill at the throat so soon to be severed by the axe, she put on an under-bodice and petticoat of crimson silk. Captivity and sorrow had long ago taken away the beauty that had become a legend in men's memories. Mary, that last morning, was middle-aged and plain. Her real hair was grey. Over it she placed her usual piled-up wig of auburn, and over that a veil of white lawn. She took a crucifix in her hand. Her rosary hung from her girdle. No one should doubt that she had died as a good Catholic.

The castle hall was crowded with noblemen and gentry and sheriff's men with gleaming helmets and halberds, all gathered to see her die. She mounted the stage and took the draped chair as if it were a throne. Many of those watching must still have been

wondering – was *she* wondering? – if even now a breathless courier would burst in, shouting that Elizabeth had revoked the sentence. They all wanted the affair to be over. But it must not be hurried. The procedure must be decently observed.

She sat while the warrant was read aloud from the parchment. Then the Dean of Peterborough begged her, even at this late hour, to give up the Catholic faith. She interrupted him. 'Peace, Master Dean,' she cried when he still went on, 'you have nothing to do with me, nor I with you.' For a time their two voices contended, the Dean loudly praying in English, Mary ignoring him and reciting the Latin she had used since childhood.

Then she was helped out of her black gown and knelt before the block, a crimson figure against the sombre background. '*In manus tuas, Domine*,' she murmured. 'Into thy hands, O Lord.' And the axe fell.

She died with the same courage and dignity as her grandson, Charles I, was to die long afterwards. She left behind her a romantic legend that has never ceased to fascinate. But the hard truth is that, though she died well, she had lived less well, and to turn her into an innocent martyr is to ignore the record of her self-willed, scheming career.

When the news reached London the bells were rung and the bonfires blazed out through the February darkness. Only Elizabeth could not share in the rejoicings. She would not eat, nor did she sleep that night.

A Long Piece of Parchment

On 10 February 1341, in the dank Thames-side town of Oxford, Robert de Eglesfield took a long piece of parchment and set down a scheme that had been dear to his heart for a long time.

The actual parchment, unusually large for such documents, measured twenty-six inches across and thirty-eight inches long. Whether Eglesfield did the writing himself or dictated it, he poured into that space a wealth of hopes and prudent precautions, for, when printed centuries later, they ran to thirty-three pages.

One might say that the parchment is longer than it looks. For it stretches much farther than its actual measurement of just over a yard. It extends across more than six hundred years of history. Its effects are still with us, and thousands of men alive today, scattered all over the world, have gained benefit from what was written on it.

Eglesfield was founding a new college. His parchment is of particular interest because he put so much detail into his plan. No earlier college possesses such fully worked-out statutes and tells us so much about university life in those days.

Eglesfield was a Cumberland man, then about forty-five. He had been for some years one of the chaplains to King Edward III's wife, that Philippa whom the chronicler Froissart described as 'the most gentle queen, the most liberal and the most courteous that ever was'.

But Eglesfield had not always been a churchman. He came of a small landowning family and he had sat in Parliament as a 'knight of the shire'. His uncle had been a clerk in the royal household – a civil servant, as we should call him today – and Eglesfield

24

had been attracted to court. So, though it was customary for such royal clerks to be in Holy Orders, and Eglesfield expressed a deep respect for the study of theology, he was a practical man, well versed in the ways of the world.

He had begun by making sure of a site for his college, buying some land and houses just off the High Street a few months before. Then he had to wait until the King came home from a campaign against the French. He had already won the goodwill of the Queen and she had agreed to lend her name to the project. Now he had only to obtain a charter from the King, perhaps slyly pointing out to him that, whereas the French had no less than thirty such colleges in Paris, Oxford had only five. At all events, the King set his seal on a charter that January, in the Tower of London, licensing Eglesfield to establish his 'hall of the Queen's scholars at Oxford', and on 10 February the statutes were put down in black and white.

There was to be a Provost at the head, and twelve Fellows, unmarried men in Holy Orders, gentle, peaceable, and fond of study. For preference they should come from Cumberland or Westmorland, but there is almost a modern ring in his phrase that they should 'exclude no race or deserving nation'. They were to wear blood-red robes in memory of Christ's death and sit on only three sides of the high table, thus imitating by their positions, as well as their number, the traditional picture of the Last Supper.

A treasurer, a steward of the hall, and a domestic bursar were to be chosen from among these Fellows, and there could be up to thirteen chaplains.

The 'Poor Boys' – the undergraduates or students as they would be called today, except that these were younger when they came – must never number more than seventy-two. They received free education in return for singing in the choir. They had four instructors, who were bidden not to spare the rod until the boys reached marriageable age. So perhaps 'Poor Boys' is a designation that may still stand.

Finally, Eglesfield laid down the domestic staff. He provided for a butler or steward, a cook and kitchen boy, a brewer (the college brewed its own beer until modern times), a miller boy to grind corn, a barber, a gardener, a washerwoman, and a night-watchman.

The canny north countryman left little to chance. The barber was to wash the Fellows' hair regularly. The washerwoman was not allowed inside the college. And the night-watchman had to go round at hourly intervals, calling the time, and to make sure that nobody overslept.

A trumpet was to be sounded when dinner was served. This regulation too (unlike some of the others) has been strictly followed throughout the centuries.

Dogs were banned. 'It is not right for poor men, especially those who are living on charity, to give the bread of the sons of men to dogs to eat.' Left-overs from meals were to be handed out to poor people at the college gate, along with pea-soup. Every day, also, thirteen persons unfit for work were to be brought into the hall itself and fed. On the day before Good Friday these men and women were also to be fitted out with russet gowns, hooded and fur-lined, and allowed to drink from the loving-cup.

Dicing and gambling were forbidden in the hall because of the quarrels they led to. Music was kept to times of relaxation, since too much of it distracted men from study.

Gentlemanly manners were to be cultivated. Eglesfield remembered his days at court where French was the language used. He decreed that, though Latin was the language spoken by scholars throughout the universities of Europe, the Queen's Fellows might talk French in hall, instead, and the boys at any time.

These and innumerable other instructions – even to the weight of the loaves to be baked – went down on the long parchment.

So was born the Queen's College at Oxford, with Queen Philippa as patroness, a role in which the queens of England have followed her ever since.

Curiously enough, the present Queen is not patroness. In Eglesfield's time it was never conceived that a woman would ever rule the country and he thought only in terms of a 'queen consort', the wife of a king. For that reason, when King George VI died, the patronage was not taken over by his daughter, Elizabeth II, but was carried on by the Queen Mother.

The Black Legion Lands in Wales

On 22 February 1797, a quiet part of the Welsh coast where nothing much had ever happened before was thrown into turmoil by the landing of armed invaders.

Such an invasion was entirely unexpected. Though Britain was at war with France, the people of Llanwnda parish, close to Fishguard in Pembrokeshire, were as surprised to see French soldiers as they would have been to encounter Martians or men from the moon.

It is easier now to understand what had happened.

Two months before, a French invasion force of more than forty vessels, carrying 15,000 troops, had evaded the British fleet and reached the shores of Ireland, where the people were expected to rise in armed rebellion and join forces with them. But adverse weather had prevented a landing, and when the wind had risen to gale pitch on Christmas Day the invaders had been forced to cut their cables, run for the open sea, and return to France.

While waiting for a chance to mount another large-scale attempt, the French decided to launch a nuisance raid on England itself. An Irish-American adventurer, Colonel Tate, was given command of a force recruited from the jails and galleys, somewhat appropriately named 'the Black Legion'. He was to sail up the Bristol Channel, burn Bristol, with special attention to its docks, magazines and other strategic features, and then to proceed through Wales to threaten Chester and Liverpool. His jail-bird followers seemed just the right sort for a mission of sabotage, though their numbers – a mere thirteen or fourteen hundred – seemed hardly adequate for such an ambitious operation. Discipline and determination might make up for the smallness of the force. The Colonel could only hope.

The Black Legion sailed from Brest on 17 February, crammed into a lugger and a corvette, with two frigates to escort them. Two days later, entering the Bristol Channel, they sighted the Dublin packet boat but let her pass, mistaking her for a warship. To compensate for this missed opportunity of a prize, they anchored off the Devon cliffs at Ilfracombe and sent a party ashore, which heroically burnt a farmhouse. Then, learning that the local volunteers, the North Devons, were mobilising against them, the landing party hastily embarked.

Tate now decided – prudently, no doubt – that the city of Bristol was too hard a nut to crack. He veered away with his little flotilla, rounded St David's Head at the southwesterly tip of Wales, and landed his troops near Fishguard. The French sea-captains, having delivered them, lost no time in sailing away in the direction of Ireland. Otherwise, they probably foresaw, they would soon have had their passengers scrambling aboard again.

At first the Welsh people did not realize that the Black Legion was much less formidable than it sounded. There was genuine alarm. The farmers hastily rounded up their cattle and sheep, loaded their belongings into wagons, and sent their wives and children into the safety of the hills. But soon the word spread that the French invaders were no more than a raggle-taggle mob put into uniform. They were not fortifying a position or preparing to advance. They were not sending out patrols, they were simply drifting about in gangs, breaking into the inns and getting hopelessly drunk.

It might be some time before regular British troops could reach this remote corner of Wales and deal with them, but, people began to ask, why wait for them? Every district had its amateur soldiers, mounted or on foot, commanded by some local

landowner. In this part of Wales there were the Castle Martin
Yeomanry, the Cardigan Militia and the Fishguard Volunteers.
Though their combined strength could not match the hundreds
of Frenchmen, these forces mustered eagerly under their own
leaders. Lord Cawdor took command, with Sir Richard Philipps
and Lord Milford to support him.

The French had been told that the country folk would welcome
them and start a revolution of their own, as some countries in
Europe had done, following the example of France. They were
taken aback when they met with no signs of friendship. Instead,
the people had fled before them, and now it looked as though a
British army was moving to attack them. Neither Tate nor his
officers had much idea of the bleak hill country in which they had
been deposited. They did not realize how far they were from any
camp or garrison, or how small were the militia bands gathering

to resist them. Their most comical miscalculation was to take the red capes then worn by Welsh women for the tunics of soldiers. The housewives of Fishguard turned out in their national costume and paraded on a distant hill. Tate concluded that they were an approaching column of 'red coats' and that he now had not a chance. That night he sent word to Lord Cawdor that he surrendered 'upon principles of humanity' and in the morning his men laid down their arms on Goodwick sands close by. The Fishguard fiasco was over.

One brawny woman, Jemima Nicholas, a cobbler by trade, had turned out with a pitchfork and is said to have taken twelve shivering French prisoners single-handed. For this feat the British Government, with a shrewd eye for propaganda, rewarded her with a pension.

The Reluctant Clergyman

'Now I shall be able to do something for Sydney Smith!' cried Lord Grey when he moved into 10 Downing Street, in 1830. But, like many other Prime Ministers before and after him, Lord Grey was better at making promises then keeping them, and when Sydney Smith died fifteen years later, on 22 February 1845, he had still never received the official recognition his many friends felt that he deserved.

Why had Lord Grey even wanted 'to do something' for him? And why should we, long afterwards, spare a moment to remember him?

Sydney Smith spent most of his life as a country parson. Such men often played a useful, if humble, part in the life of England during the eighteenth and nineteenth centuries. They were more important on the whole than they are now, but they seldom achieved any outstanding action to win a mention in the history-books.

Smith had never wanted to be a clergyman. He and his brother had been so clever at school that the other boys at Winchester had signed a protest, 'refusing to try for the College prizes if the Smiths were allowed to contend for them any more, as they always gained them'. At Oxford Sydney had wanted to go in for the Bar, where his keen brain and ready wit would have had full scope for exercise, but his father would not help him, so, like many another Oxford scholar of those days, he had little choice but to take Holy Orders. It was considered a gentlemanly occupation. The pay was low but the work was light – a lazy man needed only to take Sunday services and a burial or baptism now and again.

It did not suit the Reverend Sydney Smith. In his first parish he found himself in the wilds of Salisbury Plain. Years later he said, 'I have no relish for the country – it is a kind of healthy grave.' But he had no choice. 'Poverty is no disgrace to a man,' he observed on another occasion, 'but it is confoundedly inconvenient.'

He tried sincerely to do something to improve the bad conditions of the villagers – in his student days he had travelled in France during the French Revolution and he knew that in England too there were many things that needed to be changed. He arranged some schooling for the village children. When the squire asked him to dinner, he was so struck by Smith's brilliance – not expecting much from a young curate in such an out-of-the-way spot – that he persuaded him to become tutor to his son and go with that youth to Edinburgh University.

This was a wonderful escape. Edinburgh was a thriving intellectual centre, known as 'the Athens of the North'. Besides keeping an eye on his employer's son, Smith went to lectures on philosophy, chemistry and medicine, made a name for himself as a preacher, and won many friends.

He also found himself a wife. He could make jokes about

parsons and love, quoting the French, 'There are three sexes – men, women and clergymen,' and asking, 'How can a bishop marry? How can he flirt? The most he can say is, "I will see you in the vestry after service".' But his charm won Catherine Pybus and she married him, poor as he was, against all the opposition of her friends.

Smith made jokes about the Scots. 'It requires a surgical operation to get a joke well into a Scotch understanding,' he said. But they knew he did not always mean it. 'I never read a book before reviewing it,' he once said, 'it prejudices a man so.' If that had been really his attitude he would never have been asked to be editor of the newly-founded *Edinburgh Review*, which was to become so important a journal in the period from Wordsworth to Byron.

There was no livelihood in that, however. Its motto, said Smith wryly, should be the Latin tag meaning, 'We cultivate literature on a little oatmeal'. When his tutorial post ended, he went south with his wife to seek his fortune in London where he became known as a preacher and as a lecturer on philosophy.

His personality made him a social lion. Fashionable hostesses wanted him for their parties. His witty remarks, the more outrageous the better, were quoted everywhere.

He was the first to say, of one unfortunate lady, that she 'looked as if she had walked straight out of the Ark'. 'What you don't know,' he told someone, 'would make a great book.' Of Macaulay he said, in later years, 'He has occasional flashes of silence that make his conversation perfectly delightful.' Though he could be biting, he was not really unkind. Many of his best sayings sprang from the wildness of his fancy. 'Heat, ma'am!' he exclaimed. 'It was so dreadful that I found there was nothing left for it but to take off my flesh and sit in my bones.'

Had he been a Tory, Smith might have been made a bishop, for it lay with the Government to make the highest appointments in the Church of England. But Smith had progressive opinions – he wanted Roman Catholics to enjoy the same rights as other citizens and he stood for the reform of Parliament. The Tories were not going to promote a clergyman with such dangerous views.

Smith and his growing family had to go back to the lonely life of a country parson. From 1809 he spent twenty years at Foston in Yorkshire. No clergyman had actually lived in the parish for a century and a half. Smith had to build himself a rectory and farm 300 acres as well as performing his religious duties. The nearest neighbour with any education was seven miles away. Small wonder that Smith, starved of intellectual stimulus, found country life 'a kind of healthy grave'. But he tackled the practical problems of the parish cheerfully enough, and the villagers loved him.

He still wrote for the *Edinburgh Review*. He wrote pamphlets too on public issues, notably *Peter Plymley's Letters*, making fun of his fellow parsons who denied justice to the Catholics.

In 1828 the Tories gave him a modest appointment at Bristol Cathedral which at least allowed him to move to a parish in Somerset. But when Lord Grey and the Whigs won power two years later, and many people expected Smith to be made a bishop, he was merely made a canon of St Paul's.

At least he was able to spend the rest of his life in London, where he was happiest, and his money worries ended when he inherited £50,000 from his brother. He enjoyed life. One idea of heaven he defined as 'eating *pâtés de foie gras* to the sound of trumpets', and his couplet is often quoted:

> 'Serenely full, the epicure would say,
> Fate cannot harm me, I have dined today.'

His wit remained bright and sharp even in old age. 'I am just going to pray for you at St Paul's,' he assured someone, 'but with no very lively hope of success.'

March

Carey's Ride

In her palace at Richmond, near London, Elizabeth I lay propped upon cushions, waiting to die. In another palace, at Holyrood in Edinburgh, almost four hundred miles to the north, James VI of Scotland waited impatiently for the news that would make him also James I of England.

Meanwhile, during those chilly night hours at Richmond – for in that year, 1603, March was particularly bleak and windy – Sir Robert Carey was waiting too, eager to carry that news and make his fortune with the new monarch.

Carey was Queen Elizabeth's second cousin, related through the family of her mother, the hapless Anne Boleyn. This connection had given him a place at court but not all the advancement he wanted. Carey was thrustful and ambitious. He dressed extravagantly, beyond his modest means, and made himself noticeable as an elegant dancer and a reckless rider in tournaments. But, though now over forty, he had not risen as high as he felt he deserved.

He held a post in the wild border region of Northumberland, but he was afraid that he might lose even that when the Queen died. When James became King there would be a wholesale shuffle of public offices – and an influx of Scots. It would be every man for himself.

Carey had one advantage. James knew him and seemed to like him. Carey had performed missions to the Scottish court, used all his charm upon the King, and subsequently cultivated the connection. Now he must clinch matters with some striking service that would earn a definite reward. He aimed at becoming Lord of the Bedchamber to the King.

He had talked with the Queen when her last illness came upon her. 'No, Robin, I am not well,' she had admitted. She had pressed his hand, complaining of her weariness and depression. She had seemed so low that on 19 March he had written secretly to James, predicting that she could live only another three days.

James was getting a big postbag from England. Carey was not the only man looking ahead. The Queen's own Secretary of State, the shrewd Robert Cecil, had already drafted the proclamation announcing James's accession to the English throne. A copy, its phrases sweet to James's ear, was on its way to Edinburgh.

It was vital that the change-over should be swift and smooth. Not all Englishmen wanted a Scottish ruler and there was a real risk of trouble. For that reason Cecil and the Council planned to withhold the news of the Queen's death, when it occurred, until all was ready to proclaim her successor. The palace gates were to be shut immediately, so that no unauthorized person could get out.

Carey, however, was making his own preparations in defiance of the Privy Council. He was determined to be first at Edinburgh with the glad tidings.

He relied first upon his powerful allies inside the palace at Richmond. His brother, Lord Hunsdon, was Lord Chamberlain, and his sister, Lady Scrope, was in close attendance upon the dying Queen.

After that, he must depend on his own courage and toughness and his knowledge of the roads and travelling conditions. There he was helped by his Northumbrian connection and his previous visits to Edinburgh.

The fastest mode of travel was to 'ride post', changing to a fresh hired horse every ten miles or so. The system was well established along the principal roads. One paid so much a mile, and each beast, after a rest, could be ridden back to its own posting-house by the next traveller in the reverse direction. With special planning (and Carey had done some of that) one could sometimes arrange extra changes of horse in the middle of a stage, and so be able to ride at an even more furious pace.

The whole notion appealed to Carey's sporting instincts. Years before, as a young man, he had won a bet of £2,000 by walking to Berwick in twelve days. Now he was playing for an even larger stake.

One thing he had underestimated – the old Queen's hold on life. She lingered until the fifth day. On 24 March, about three o'clock in the morning, she died quietly in her sleep. Lady Scrope slipped away from the death-bed and handed her brother the blue sapphire ring from the Queen's finger – a ring which James himself had given her. The return of that ring was to be the token that she was dead.

By now the exits from the palace were bolted and guarded. But the great officers of state, like the Lord Chamberlain, must clearly pass to and fro upon their urgent business. Lord Hunsdon walked out, and his brother followed at his heels, unchallenged by the sentries. Safe outside, Carey mounted a waiting horse and rode through the darkness to London. There he waited a little while, because there was a chance that the Privy Council might appoint him their official messenger. But he was warned that they would only trick him into delay, so without further loss of time he started.

The state of the roads in 1603 defies modern imagination. There had been no systematic construction, with foundations, drainage and surfacing, since the departure of the Romans twelve centuries before. Bridges were kept up, often by tolls or charity funds, but little was done to repair the highways between. Wagons and coaches gouged deep ruts. Potholes and hollows filled with rainwater. To ride at speed after dark was suicidal.

How fast could Carey cover the journey? Once a mayor of Exeter had ridden to London in four days, which had been reckoned a short time, but the distance, 172 miles, had been much less than half what Carey had to travel. In the Middle Ages a King's Messenger had taken ten days from London to Lancaster, and thirteen days to come back. Neither roads nor horses had improved since then.

This is what makes Carey's achievement remarkable.

By nightfall of that first day, Thursday, 24 March, he was at Doncaster, 163 miles north of London.

All through Friday he rode like a maniac, pausing only to snatch a mouthful of food and drink as he slid from the saddle of one steaming beast and mounted another. That night he reached his own house at Widdrington, seven miles beyond Morpeth, and allowed himself a brief rest.

By noon on Saturday he was over the Scottish border with less than sixty miles to go. He would not fail now. He would be at Holyrood, he told himself, before dark.

It was now that disaster almost overcame him. His horse fell. He was thrown clear, but not quite clear enough. One hoof caught him a glancing blow on the head. Dizzy, faint with loss of blood, almost at the limit of his endurance, he clambered into the saddle and rode slowly on again.

Those last few dozen miles seemed endless. Only his iron will

39

kept him going. To have come so far, so fast, and then to be cheated of his prize, was unthinkable.

In his Edinburgh palace the King sighed and prepared for bed. It was nearly midnight. There would be no news now. Like as not, the old Queen was still alive. She would go on teasing them all as she had done throughout the forty-five years of her reign.

There was a flurry in the doorway. James, ever fearful of assassination, was most carefully guarded. But a travel-stained figure, his hair caked with blood, was allowed to stumble into the room and fall on one knee. He held out a hand. In the flickering candle-light gleamed a sapphire ring.

Carey got his appointment as a Lord of the Bedchamber. He had earned it. He did not, in fact, hold it for long – but he had made good his foothold in the new court. A man of Carey's type was not to be kept down. Doggedly, throughout James's reign, he took care of his own interests. But he had to wait for Charles I to become King in 1625 before he achieved the summit of his career, when Charles made him, a year later, Earl of Monmouth.

Palm Sunday at Scone

Nine years earlier, King Edward I of England had carried away the famous Stone of Scone on which all Scottish kings had been crowned since time immemorial. That made no difference. It was to Scone that Robert the Bruce made his way on Palm Sunday, 27 March 1306, to hoist his royal standard in defiance of the English and to assume the crown of Scotland.

In a second ceremony, two days later, Isobel, Countess of Fife, claimed the traditional right to place that crown on his head again.

It should have been done by her brother, representing the MacDuff clan, but he was afraid. Scornfully, she took his place.

There was some excuse for her brother. Edward, well-named 'the Hammer of the Scots', had been ruthless in his efforts to bring the northern kingdom under his own control. He had worn down the resistance of the patriots, captured their leader, Sir William Wallace, and savagely executed him in London the previous year. It needed a brave man to continue the struggle.

Robert the Bruce came of Norman ancestry, so that in blood he was closely related to the English nobility south of the border. It is said that he spent much of his youth at the English court and he was no foreigner there. Nor, in the earlier part of his life, did he oppose King Edward, but served under him in various capacities with every sign of loyalty and contentment.

The Scots themselves had been unable to agree as to who should be their rightful king, and Edward had played off one party against another so that he himself should be the real master of the country. Robert was one of the claimants. Early in 1306 matters came to a head, and he saw that his only hope was to come out boldly as the leader of the resistance to England – to be a true King of Scotland, not a puppet whose strings were pulled from Westminster.

Edward's answer was a hammer-stroke worthy of his nickname. He sent his army northwards. Late in June the Scottish forces were smashed at Methven. Some of Robert's chief followers were hanged, drawn and quartered. The brave Countess of Fife was punished for crowning him. Like Robert's wife, daughter and sister, she was taken prisoner, though the story that she was kept in an iron cage at Berwick Castle is probably untrue. Three of Robert's brothers were killed. Only he himself remained at liberty, an outlaw in the hills. It is to this period that the legend of 'Bruce and the Spider' belongs, telling how the dejected fugitive hid in a cave and learnt patience from watching the spider at work.

The spider's example was a sound one. Although everything seemed so hopeless at that time, the Palm Sunday coronation had set the Scottish king on a road that led to victory.

Palm Sunday of the following year brought the turn of the tide. His right-hand man, Sir James Douglas, the renowned 'Black Douglas', recaptured his own Douglas Castle on that day, and, knowing that he could not prevent the English from re-occupying it, destroyed it without hesitation.

Scottish hopes revived. More and more men rallied to the cause. Several successes were won, and Edward, though unwell, marched northwards in person with a large army to settle the matter once and for all. It is difficult to say what would have happened if Edward had lived. But on 7 July he died, and though he bequeathed the struggle to his son, Edward II, that monarch was not the type of man to carry it to victory.

The war, however, dragged on, waged with horrible savagery on both sides. Robert gradually spread his control over most of Scotland, driving out every English garrison except the one at Stirling, and carrying the fight into northern England, where he sacked Durham and laid waste the countryside.

It was near Stirling, at Bannockburn, in 1314, that he faced Edward II and routed his army, though it vastly outnumbered the Scots.

After that, Robert's power seemed secure, though he was not recognized by the English and the two countries remained at war. King Edward asked the Pope to confirm the excommunication a previous Pope had pronounced against Robert, but a strong declaration by the nobility, clergy and people of Scotland persuaded His Holiness to remove the ban instead.

'We fight,' they said stoutly, 'not for glory, nor riches, nor honour, but only for that liberty which no true man relinquishes but with his life.' Robert was their rightful king 'by the providence of God, by the right of succession, by those laws and customs which we are resolved to defend even with our lives, and by our own just consent . . . Yet Robert himself, should he turn aside from the task he has begun and yield Scotland or us to the English king or his people, we should cast out as an enemy of us all, and we should choose another king to defend our freedom. For so long as a hundred remain alive we are minded never a whit to bow beneath the yoke of English dominion.'

Robert did not betray their faith in him. He rebuffed every attack and took the fight into England and Ireland. The English wearied at last, and in 1328 a treaty was signed at Northampton, acknowledging the independence of Scotland and Robert as her lawful sovereign.

It had been a long hard road from that crowning at Scone twenty-two years earlier, and Robert enjoyed his final triumph for little more than a year. In June 1329, he died.

A Remarkable Elopement

Duels and elopements form the very stuff of eighteenth-century romances – Sheridan's comedy, *The Rivals*, is a famous example – but no play or novel surpasses the tale of Sheridan's own elopement on the night of Wednesday, 18 March 1772.

The setting (like that of *The Rivals*) was the city of Bath, then at the height of its Georgian elegance. Richard Brinsley Sheridan was twenty. His widowed father, an Irish actor and writer, had moved there a year before with his two sons and two daughters, and had rented a house in Kingsmead Street.

Soon afterwards, the Sheridans had been invited to a musical party at the home of Thomas Linley, a composer and singer who promoted concerts in Bath. There was a large family of young Linleys, brilliantly talented and – boys and girls alike – extraordinarily good-looking.

Elizabeth Ann was the eldest, only sixteen, but already famous. She sang the principal soprano parts at her father's concerts and had appeared in London at Covent Garden. The great artist Gainsborough, who lived in Bath, had painted her portrait.

Her beauty caused her to be pestered with suitors. In 1771, to her embarrassment, she was made the subject of a quite libellous play by Samuel Foote, produced at the Haymarket in London under the title of *The Maid of Bath*, the nickname she had been given by her admiring public.

This play contained a caricature of Elizabeth's mother. It also introduced a 'Major Thomas Rackett', recognizable by everyone as a certain Thomas Mathews, who had recently married and settled in Bath, and who was known as 'Captain' Mathews though he had no claim to the rank. Mathews had tired of his Welsh wife and had fallen in love with Elizabeth Linley. He was making her miserable with his attentions. Sometimes he frightened her with threats of suicide. She was afraid too lest her father should hear of his behaviour and feel bound to challenge Mathews to a duel, in which he would be no match for the 'Captain'.

Early in 1772 the girl had reached the end of her tether. More and more she disliked the publicity of the concert platform and all the gossip – however flattering – about her charms and her countless admirers.

She longed to escape from it all. As she had once told her father, when discussing her career as a singer, 'If I did marry, I should marry to be *free*.'

Now she poured out her troubles to Alicia Sheridan, who was nineteen and of an age to understand. Mr Sheridan was away from home, fulfilling theatrical engagements in his native Dublin. The household in Kingsmead Street was temporarily reduced to Richard and his two young sisters.

Elizabeth Linley said she would like to run away to France and seek refuge in a convent until she was twenty-one and able to manage her own affairs.

Alicia had friends in France, at St Quentin, and offered to help with letters of introduction. Richard declared that a girl could not possibly make such a journey alone. He would escort her.

So the remarkable 'elopement' was planned, with no word of love or marriage between the two. Richard even engaged a woman (whose identity is not recorded) to go with them as chaperon.

That Wednesday evening most of the Linleys were performing at a concert. Elizabeth said she was unwell and her father excused her. At the appointed time Richard appeared at their house in the Crescent with one of the curtained sedan-chairs in which ladies were often carried through the dark and muddy streets. Thus concealed, Elizabeth reached the London road, where she found the chaperon waiting in a post-chaise. Richard handed her in and took his own seat in the carriage. They were off.

They reached London early the next morning, having travelled through the night. They had not much money and were thankful to get a free passage across the sea to Dunkirk through the kindness of a friend's father, a brandy importer. But the weather was wild, and Elizabeth was so sick that Richard was afraid she would die.

Until now, their friendship had been restricted by the conventions of the time. The excitements and hardships of the past day or two quickly produced a new closeness between them. When they had travelled on from Dunkirk to Calais, Richard announced that he had loved her all along and had come with the hope of marrying her. And Elizabeth, moved by his consideration and chivalry, quickly agreed.

They found a priest, who probably specialized in such runaway matches. He performed a ceremony which was quite without legal force, since they were Protestants and under age. But it served for the moment.

Elizabeth still kept to her scheme of lodging in a convent, but it proved difficult to arrange. She stayed a few nights with the nuns, then, falling ill again, moved into the house of a kindly English doctor and his wife. On recovering, she joined Richard at a hotel, and there after a little while her father arrived to fetch her home.

The French 'marriage', not being valid, was kept secret, and for a whole year the stern Mr Linley insisted on the couple remaining separate. Not until 13 April 1773 were they united at Marylebone Church and allowed to begin their happy married life together.

Before that, Richard had fought a duel with the rascally Mathews, who had inserted an insulting announcement about him in the *Bath Chronicle*. They fought by candlelight in a London tavern. Richard disarmed the 'Captain' and snapped his sword in two. Mathews first conceded defeat, shouting, 'I beg my life', and then complained that he had been unfairly beaten. He was offered the chance to fight a second duel, with pistols, but declined. Finally, still blustering, he had to make a written apology, which was promptly published in the Bath newspaper.

Richard, hot-blooded, romantic and chivalrous though he was, never lost his sense of humour. Within a year or two of these stirring events he was transmuting some of his experiences into the high-spirited comedy of *The Rivals*, which was produced at Covent Garden in January 1775, when he was only twenty-three, and quickly took its place among the masterpieces of English drama.

A Contract for Charcoal

Much history is buried in dull-looking legal documents of long ago. Stirring the dust of centuries we catch glimpses of ordinary folk, nobodies who are now themselves dust, names that would otherwise have perished utterly. For a moment they live again, and we see them at their work.

So, from an ancient charter that belonged to Fountains Abbey in Yorkshire and is now preserved in the Bodleian Library at Oxford, we know that in March 1195, in the middle of Richard Lionheart's short reign, a certain William de Stutevill made an agreement with the master smith of that great Cistercian monastery.

The smith needed vast quantities of wood to produce charcoal for the heating of his forge. William owned forest land at Knaresborough not far away. He gave the smith permission to burn charcoal there, 'where and how much as he may will of dead wood whether standing or lying . . . in perfect peace and . . . free from all hindrance'. In exchange, the smith undertook to pay a rent of ten shillings per annum and supply William with sixty horseshoes, and, starting from Easter of that year, he could burn charcoal on those terms for as long as he pleased.

To avoid any possible misunderstanding or unpleasantness, William then wrote – or more probably dictated to a clerk – 'to the bailiffs and foresters of Knaresborough . . . greeting', telling them what had been settled.

Charcoal-burning was an important feature of English life until coal, and then coke, became available for making iron and other purposes. In one part alone of the great Forest of Dean in Gloucestershire nearly nine hundred hearths or pits were counted in 1282. It was largely due to this wholesale destruction of woodlands that the forests of England were so diminished by Stuart

times, for even if the smith at Fountains Abbey kept to his bargain with William of Stutevill and burned only dead wood, not all men were so scrupulous.

Charcoal-burning was a skilled craft and those who followed it tended to become rather a race apart, passing down their technical knowledge from father to son, and living their own separate existence in the woods.

They built up a domed pile of logs, hollow inside and roofed with turf, sand or soil, and with screens to control the air-flow to the heart of the fire. The art was in the slow combustion. The pile had to burn for five whole days and nights, and during that period the men had to 'live rough' in the forest so that they were always on hand to tend it. That is probably why, in old stories, it is so often a charcoal-burner's hut that provides shelter when someone gets lost in the wilderness.

It is not very likely that the master smith of Fountains would personally quit his forge to camp out in this fashion. He made the agreement with William, but he was probably far too important a monastery servant to do such work himself.

Operation, Celebration

Early in 1658 Samuel Pepys faced the unpleasant truth. There was nothing for it, he must undergo an operation.

In those days it was a dreadful risk, a gamble with death against heavy odds. There had been surgery since ancient times, some of it remarkably dexterous, but only a very few operations were attempted, such as the amputation of arms and legs after a battle when there was no other possible treatment, and the death-rate afterwards was alarmingly high.

By 1658 men had at least emerged from the dark superstitions of the Middle Ages. A scientific attitude was developing. Surgeons knew a good deal about anatomy, the circulation of the blood, and some at least of the other workings of the body. But they knew nothing about germs or the importance of keeping their instruments scrupulously clean, as well as the patient's wound. Antiseptics were unknown, and many sufferers died of infections following the operation. Nor had the surgeon any effective anaesthetic to prevent pain and shock. The most he could do was to make the patient drowsy with drink or some kind of concoction, and then, having enlisted some strong helpers to hold him down, do the job with lightning speed.

It was not a prospect that any man could face without blenching, and Pepys, then just twenty-five, was never one of the bravest. Timid by nature, a prey of fears and forebodings, he nonetheless had a wonderful gift for screwing up his courage when he had to, and rising to the occasion. He did so now.

Since his student days at Cambridge he had suffered much pain, off and on, from a 'stone' formed in his kidney and causing an obstruction. This complaint was common, and the removal of such stones by surgery was one of the few operations regularly carried out. This at least meant that the surgeons were skilful and experienced – they could make the incision and extract the stone inside two minutes – but the risk and pain were still considerable.

Pepys's father introduced him to a surgeon who specialized in this 'lithotomy' as it was called, a Thomas Hollier of St Thomas's Hospital. Dr Moleyns, of St Bartholomew's, prescribed a soothing draught compounded of rose water, white of egg, liquorice and other ingredients, which may have comforted the patient beforehand but probably did not do much to render him unaware of the pain.

The operation took place on 26 March, not at the hospital but (as usual in those days) at a private house. Pepys's home had no suitable room. Not only was space needed for the surgeon and his assistants, but all the patient's relatives were expected to crowd round, partly to give him moral support and partly to be handy to say farewell if, as so frequently happened, he succumbed. On this occasion a kind relative, Mrs Turner, offered accommodation in her house close by, just off Fleet Street.

All went well. Mr Hollier worked with the deftness of a conjuror and produced, from Pepys's pain-racked interior, a stone weighing two ounces. Pepys made a good recovery, and for the rest of his life, whenever 26 March came round, he gave a thanksgiving dinner party, not forgetting to invite Mrs Turner. The stone he kept in a case specially made for it. He liked to pass it round as an exhibit, partly to demonstrate the ordeal he had survived and partly to encourage afflicted friends to risk a similar operation.

Posterity might well join in Pepys's celebration. Had things gone otherwise that day, there would never have been the *Diary* to delight us.

April

The Pilgrim Season

'When in April the sweet showers fall . . .' begins Chaucer's
Canterbury Tales in the sprightly modern English version by
Nevill Coghill, and the poet goes on to describe the spring-
time weather when the world is coming to life again after the
harsh winter:

> 'And the small fowl are making melody
> That sleep away the night with open eye
> (So nature pricks them and their heart engages)
> Then people long to go on pilgrimages.'

Chaucer was writing about 1387, but he was describing a custom
of making pilgrimages which had gone on for centuries and was
to continue long after his time.

Originally, the idea of pilgrimages was entirely religious. A
man wanted to show that he was genuinely penitent for some sin:
he vowed (or was positively ordered by the Church) to make a
long, difficult, even dangerous journey to some holy place such
as the tomb of a saint. In the same way, he might wish to give
thanks for recovery from an illness, or he might hope that recovery
would follow if he made the pilgrimage first. And a man, or a
woman, might be so devout by nature that, though neither ill
nor guilty of any grave sin, they could think of no worthier
occupation than moving on from one sacred shrine to another,
praying at each and fixing their minds on higher things.

After a study of Chaucer's twenty-nine Canterbury pilgrims,
all so delightfully different in character and motive, it is obvious
that only a small proportion were deeply pious in this way. The

Wife of Bath, for example, who was actually a widow and a very merry widow at that, had worn out five husbands and had clearly joined the party with an idea at the back of her mind that she might pick up a sixth.

For her, and for a large proportion of the other pilgrims who took to the roads each April, it was something suspiciously like what in modern times is called the 'holiday season'.

In the Middle Ages there was nothing else equivalent to our habit of taking holidays. A holiday, or 'holy day', was simply a break from work in honour of a church festival. There were plenty of those, dotted through the year, but for ordinary folk there was no question of going away from home for a week or longer and enjoying oneself in some distant place. Most people passed their whole lives without stirring more than a few miles from the parish where they were born.

Always, however, human nature being what it is, there were restless, curious, adventurous types who wanted to travel and see strange sights. For such persons a pilgrimage was the one respectable excuse that everyone could understand. So each year, when the winter was over and the roads fit for journeys, the itch came upon them to be off.

Those who made pilgrimages for their health probably derived benefit. The fresh air and exercise would in many cases do them good. So would the change of scene and company if they were suffering from mental depression. And if something was on their conscience, the psychological effect of doing something so definite must have been a relief. Not knowing any more scientific reason for feeling better, they gave the credit to the saints they prayed to, and to the bottles of holy water and other souvenirs they brought back.

Perhaps the oddest motive of all was to annoy the King or his government. Medieval people could not vote or write letters to the newspapers and, when they tried a protest march, they were apt to be ridden down by armed men. But if a popular leader was killed (like Simon de Montfort), they could show their disapproval by going in large numbers to his tomb, though he might have been anything but a saint. Thomas, Earl of Lancaster, was not a very good character, but when he was beheaded by Edward II pilgrims flocked to his tomb at Pontefract until the Archbishop of York was at his wits' end to know how to stop them. Strangely enough, when King Edward himself (a far from saintly man) was murdered a few years afterwards, *his* tomb at Gloucester also became a popular place of pilgrimage. The Gloucester monks made a very good thing out of the offerings, the sale of souvenirs, and the provision of food and accommodation.

There was money in pilgrimages. There were hostels and guest-houses all along the road, often managed by the monasteries. Inns and taverns did a roaring trade. Tolls, ferries, hirers of horses and boats, traders of every sort, all derived benefit. So did the numerous pickpockets, swindlers, and other dishonest characters who attached themselves to the travellers. There were not many really poor pilgrims. Those who undertook the enterprise at all usually had money in their purses.

And they were out for a good time. They travelled in groups, like Chaucer's twenty-nine, not only for protection against

robbers but for the pleasure of company. They liked to sing as they rode, not necessarily hymns but more often (as William Thorpe complained in 1407) 'wanton songs', and any pilgrim who could play the bagpipes was particularly welcome.

When they reached their destination, they took care to buy the appropriate badge which proved they had been there – a tiny image of St Thomas from Canterbury, or, if they had been much farther afield, a scallop from Compostella in Spain or a palm from the Holy Land. These badges were of lead or pewter, pierced with a hole so that they could be stitched on one's hood or cape. Regular pilgrims could display a row of such emblems. It was sometimes whispered that certain boastful members of the party had not been to as many shrines as they pretended.

In England, besides Canterbury, some of the most popular shrines were those of Our Lady of Walsingham in Norfolk (her statue was said to work miracles), St Hugh at Lincoln, St Edmund in Suffolk, St Cuthbert at Durham, St David in Wales, and the Holy Thorn at Glastonbury. A few weeks were needed for one of these journeys, but for Rome one allowed sixteen weeks and for Jerusalem a whole year. That last pilgrimage was a formidable adventure indeed, but enough people undertook it to create a regular industry. Pilgrim-ships sailed from Venice, guides and interpreters were available, and even the most inexperienced traveller – if his purse was heavy enough – could have most things arranged for him.

Not only had the pilgrim traffic developed into something remarkably like the modern tourist industry, but there were even, in some cases, the beginnings of the 'package tour'.

The Truth About Macbeth

One cannot honestly say that, when April comes round, many people's thoughts fly to that April of 1057, when Malcolm III was crowned King of Scotland on the historic stone of Scone, following the defeat of Macbeth.

Nonetheless, as Shakespeare's *Macbeth* ranks among the greatest and best-known plays ever written, it is interesting to recall its hero, round about the anniversary of his death, and compare the facts of his life with the theatrical fiction.

Shakespeare was no historian. He was quite happy to take a good plot from someone else's book, in this case the *Chronicle of Scottish History* by an Elizabethan writer, Raphael Holinshed, and then to turn it into a play without checking it for accuracy.

So, thanks to Shakespeare's genius – the acting of his drama all over the modern world and the study of it in schools and colleges – everyone thinks of Macbeth as an ambitious tyrant, egged on by a ruthless wife to murder an innocent old king and usurp his throne. What were the real events leading up to that final battle in the Highlands and the burial of Macbeth under the cairn that still bears his name, outside Lumphanan village, twenty-five miles from Aberdeen?

At this date, when England was under her last Anglo-Saxon kings and the Norman Conquest was close at hand, Scotland was a disunited and confused country in which the numerous Gaelic clans warred with each other and with the Viking raiders, the English in the south and the Celts of the Strathclyde. There was no permanent border. Sometimes Cumberland and Northumberland formed part of Scotland, and at other times the English pushed their dominion as far north as Edinburgh.

Duncan became king in 1034, but to many Scots *he* was the usurper, not Macbeth who overthrew him in 1040. Macbeth's wife, Gruach, was of royal blood, and because of that he was able to make out a claim to the throne which many thought reasonable, especially since, as the ruler or 'Mormaer' of Moray, he was the natural leader of the northern Picts, who made up a big part of the population.

Whatever the legal rights or wrongs – uncertain then, and quite undiscoverable by now – Macbeth reigned for seventeen years, not as the bloody dictator portrayed by Shakespeare but (according to St Berchan) as a good king who made Scotland prosperous. He was a benefactor of the Church and in 1050 made the long pilgrimage to Rome. This may have indicated that he had something on his conscience (though not necessarily) but if he had really been a hated tyrant he would scarcely have dared to leave his kingdom for such a lengthy absence.

There were, however, constant plots against him. He seems to have had no heir to succeed him, though Gruach, who had been married before, had a son Lulach by her first husband, Gilcomgain. This explains the mysterious reference in Shakespeare, where Lady Macbeth implies that she has been a mother, though no child of Macbeth appears. In 1054 the Earl of Northumbria, a gigantic Dane named Siward (a character in the play), invaded Scotland to help Duncan's elder son, Malcolm. He defeated Macbeth, but, it is interesting to note, did not topple him from his throne. It was not until three years later that, Siward having died in the meantime, Malcolm (nicknamed 'Canmore' or 'Large-head') achieved the final victory by his own efforts.

The Bishop Disapproved

If, by some scientific device enabling us to view across time as well as space, we could focus on any English village on Monday, 13 April 1450, we might well be puzzled to understand what came up on our screen.

What are they doing, these laughing housewives and girls in the long skirts and aprons, the wimples and kerchiefs of Henry V I's reign, stretching ropes across the street and driving into a corner that unfortunate fellow who has chosen the wrong moment to pass by?

All is well. He has groped in his pouch and handed over a coin. They have let him go – but now the whole pack have swung round, giggling as the miller's wife trips over the slack rope, and they are off in the other direction in shrill pursuit of another man.

What is it all in aid of?

It is quite literally 'in aid' of something, for this is Hock Monday, the second Monday after Easter, when from time immemorial the women have gone 'hocking', allowed to catch any male passer-by with their ropes and extract a donation from him for parish purposes. Tomorrow, on Hock Tuesday, it will be the men's turn to do the chasing and the women's turn to walk warily or stay indoors, unless of course they enjoy the fun of being chased.

The meaning of the word 'Hock' is unknown, but Hocktide was an important date in the year because it was the time when rents were paid, as at Michaelmas six months later. It fell in April except in those years when Easter was especially late, and the 'hocking' provided an excuse for a little fun in the quiet days between the Easter festival and the full-scale junketings of May Day. Though medieval people had no bank holidays, their year was full of occasions like this which made a break from the toil of farm and workshop.

The money collected in forfeits was very useful too. There were not all the elaborate rates and taxes, grants and subsidies, we know today. Each parish was largely a self-contained unit, paying its own way without help from a national or local government department.

But there were always people who disapproved of raising the money in this light-hearted manner – just as they disapproved of the 'church-ales', a popular way of collecting funds by holding a party, which was apt to become more riotous than the churchwardens intended.

So, in 1450, the Bishop of Worcester issued an order that Hocktide should not be observed in the parishes of his diocese. He was not having any of this nonsense, this chasing of men by women and women by men, which might lead to no end of misbehaviour.

How much difference His Lordship's edict made is not recorded. It is fair to be supposed that in many a Worcestershire village, far from the Bishop's eye, the fun and games went on much as before, whether or not any money found its way into the parish funds.

In some parts of England the Hocktide customs were kept up until the beginning of the eighteenth century.

In Quest of a Continent

Four black men, fishing in the bay from their small bark canoes, took not the slightest notice as the ship, her spread canvas bright in the afternoon sun, came gliding majestically between the two headlands into the sheltered haven. They completed their fishing, paddled shorewards with their catch, and ate it with their families by the camp-fire as if nothing had happened.

Yet that ship – the first they had ever seen in their lives and which they ignored as though it were no more than a giant white butterfly – had brought the first white men, the men who were going in a short time to take their country from them and jerk it out of the Stone Age into the modern world, adding a continent to the map, and in due course another English-speaking nation to mankind.

The date was 29 April 1770. The ship was the *Endeavour*, a roomy Whitby collier adapted for Pacific exploration, and commanded by Lieutenant James Cook, R.N., who had often served in such craft before entering the service of King George III. And the place was, for the moment, nameless. But we should look for it today in the southern suburbs of Sydney, at Kurnell, where an obelisk marks the spot.

Cook was in search of another continent that men had long believed in, but which in fact did not exist – Terra Australis, 'the southern land', imagined as stretching between the uncharted waters of the South Pacific and the Pole. Earlier navigators had discovered the northern and northwestern coasts of what is now called 'Australia' – *they*, being Dutchmen, named it 'New Holland' – but it was not until Cook and his British expedition

came groping their way across the unknown sea and sighted the eastern coast (later to be New South Wales) that the extent of the vast island was revealed.

Cook had been coasting northwards for over a week, baffled by the endless line of surf, when at last an inlet offered a passage into calm water and a chance to land.

As soon as the *Endeavour* was anchored, Cook ordered a couple of boats to be lowered, their crews fully armed. For, though the fishermen had taken no notice of the ship, other aborigines had been sighted carrying spears and what looked like short curved swords, but came to be known as boomerangs.

As the boats drew near the shore, two of these armed black men came down to the water's edge, shouting angrily and indicating that the strangers should go back.

Cook, a kindly man, was reluctant to provoke a fight, but he was in some difficulty. He needed fresh water for his crew and he was under Admiralty orders to explore unmapped territory of this sort. He had with him a man from Tahiti, named Tupia, who had proved a useful interpreter with the Maoris of New Zealand a few weeks earlier. But these broad-featured aborigines looked quite different from the Maoris, and clearly did not understand a word that Tupia said.

Peaceful gestures were tried. Gifts were held out. The black men stood their ground and looked more fierce than ever. Shots were fired over their heads, but these meant no more than noise and smoke – never having met fire-arms, they could not imagine the bullets that flew invisibly through the air.

In the end, to avoid a hand-to-hand struggle in which someone might have been killed, Cook was forced to load with small shot, pellets suitable for game but incapable of wounding a man badly at such long range. Even when peppered with these, the aborigines still barred the landing. It was only after several shots that they ran away into the trees.

Advancing cautiously, the sailors found a number of huts and some children whom the fugitives had not carried off with them. To show that no harm was intended, Cook set out a number of trifling presents, beads, nails, combs and looking-glasses, which had proved popular with other Pacific peoples. But he learned afterwards that the aborigines, when they crept back to their homes, had not even touched his offerings. They had no use for them. They were utterly indifferent to the material civilization of the white man.

For a week the *Endeavour* lay at anchor, while explorations were made on shore without any further conflict with the inhabitants. The place had to be named. Cook was inclined to call it Stingray Harbour, for the water was full of those dangerous fishes, but finally the name chosen was 'Botany Bay', because the immediate surroundings were so rich in plants unfamiliar to the scientists in the party.

These were headed by Joseph Banks, a wealthy young amateur botanist, already at twenty-seven a Fellow of the Royal Society, who had managed to join the expedition through his friendship with the First Lord of the Admiralty. It would not have been surprising if Banks and Cook had been at loggerheads, for the naval lieutenant, by contrast, had come up the hard way. The son of a Yorkshire farm labourer, he had been a grocer's boy before shipping aboard the colliers that carried coal to London from the northeastern ports. Then, having mastered navigation, he had gone to the bottom of the ladder again by enlisting in the Royal Navy as an ordinary seaman and earning a commission by sheer merit.

So he might well have looked down his nose at the gentleman scientist. But in fact the men had become great friends during the long voyage, for Banks was a thorough sportsman, good-tempered, uncomplaining, and entirely unspoilt by the easy and luxurious life his class enjoyed in Georgian England. Also, though he had little success with the Australian aborigines, he usually got on very well with the Pacific islanders they encountered elsewhere.

Banks had his way. 'Botany Bay' the harbour was duly named – and that name passed into history with grim associations, for in most people's minds it came to mean the place to which convicts were shipped from England, often for the rest of their lives.

Oddly enough, very few of those criminals ever saw Botany Bay. When Governor Phillip came out, eighteen years later, with the first shipload of hapless prisoners, he decided that the place was unsuitable. He stayed just one week. Then he moved up the coast a few miles and established his settlement where Sydney now stands.

No subsequent parties went to Botany Bay. But the name stuck ever afterwards, and most people mistakenly still think of that quiet haven as a place that witnessed many years of human misery.

The Birthday

Several anniversaries fall on 23 April. It was the day in 1915 when the handsome young poet, Rupert Brooke, died on the eve of the assault on Gallipoli and was buried on Achilles' fabled Greek island of Scyros. Exactly three years later, in the same World War I, it saw a daring British naval exploit, the Zeebrugge raid, when a landing party blew up the exit used by German destroyers and submarines. And 23 April is St George's Day, when churches fly the old English flag, a red cross on a white field, in honour of the country's patron saint.

But the English (unlike the Scots, Welsh and Irish) do not pay much regard to their saint, and the anniversary most honoured is one often known quite simply as 'the Birthday', without saying whose. For that not only the English flag flies but the flags of almost every nation in the world, and the ambassadors of those nations walk in procession through the streets of Stratford-upon-Avon, saluting the memory of William Shakespeare.

It is not absolutely certain that Shakespeare *was* born on that date but the parish register records his baptism on 26 April 1564, and it was usual for children then to be christened very soon after birth, because so many died in infancy. Shakespeare's parents had already had two girls, Joan and Margaret, but both had died, so no time would be lost in arranging William's baptism. There is no doubt whatever that he *died* on 23 April 1616, and there is a strong tradition that it was his fifty-second birthday.

It was a short life by modern reckoning, but it was long enough to span the whole period of the Elizabethan drama, one of the greatest ages of play-writing in the history of the theatre. And it was long enough for Shakespeare himself to produce a body of literary work which in richness, variety and power is still unsurpassed. He wrote at least thirty-six plays – it sounds odd not to be exact, but playwrights often worked together or adapted other works, like modern scriptwriters, and it is not always possible to allocate the 'credits' to every lesser-known piece. Besides the plays – tragedies like *Hamlet* and *Macbeth*, comedies like *A Midsummer Night's Dream* and *As You Like It*, histories like *Richard II* and *Henry V* – he wrote long poems, such as *Venus and Adonis*, and well over a hundred sonnets.

So few facts are known for certain about his life that many people have written books to argue that Shakespeare was not really the author of the plays that bear his name. If he was, they say, we should know more about him. But it is fair to remember that in those days very few records were kept, there were no articles and interviews on television, and there was no fashion for biographies and autobiographies of living people. Another famous playwright, Christopher Marlowe, was born in the same year as Shakespeare, and his life too is full of gaps and question-marks, but no one finds it difficult to believe that he wrote his plays.

Marlowe got off the mark more quickly than Shakespeare. Coming down from Cambridge, a university intellectual and an ardent poet, Marlowe took the rough-and-ready verse-form used by the actors of his day and hammered it into a keen and supple instrument, the unrhymed 'blank verse' with five beats to a line which sounds close to natural speech yet has (because of its subtle rhythm) a heightened emotional effect. Marlowe was famous and dead – mysteriously murdered – almost before Shakespeare had made much progress. Shakespeare carried on where Marlowe left off. He still further improved blank verse, and he poured into his plays a deeper knowledge of the world and of men than Marlowe had lived to gain, together with a practical stage-craft in which Marlowe had little interest.

For Marlowe was pure poet, and did not act himself. Shakespeare, on the other hand, came up the hard way, never studying

65

at a university but joining a company of players and in time becoming one of the main shareholders. He seems to have acted in secondary parts and made himself a valued and dependable member of the team, first by revising and polishing up old scripts by other authors, and then by turning out new plays as required, sometimes (as in the case of *Twelfth Night*) commissioned for special occasions.

There was no proper system of copyright and performing fees. Shakespeare was paid for a new play, but not much. He made his money as a 'sharer' with all the other regular actors who formed the company. It was his savings from this source, not his royalties from writing, that enabled him to buy a fine house (New Place) in his home town of Stratford, and to retire there in 1610. He still kept up his financial interest in the London theatre, and went up there from time to time, but it was in the Stratford house that he died six years later, and his tomb, visited by countless visitors every year, is in Stratford parish church, beside the River Avon which also glides past the Memorial Theatre where his plays are still acted at the annual festival.

May

Dunkirk: The Way Out

'We are beaten, we have lost the battle.' It was the voice of the French Prime Minister, Paul Reynaud, speaking in English and in great agitation over the telephone from Paris.

Winston Churchill grunted and frowned. It was half-past seven in the morning, 15 May 1940, and he had been specially woken to take the urgent call, his normal habit being to work late at night and sleep on.

'Surely it can't have happened so soon?' he objected.

'The front is broken near Sedan,' insisted Reynaud. 'They are pouring through in great numbers – tanks and armoured cars!'

So began perhaps the grimmest month that Britain had ever had to face.

The Second World War had opened in the previous September, with Hitler's surprise attack on Poland and swift overrunning of that country with Russian connivance. But there had been no real fighting elsewhere until a month ago, when there had been another German surprise attack, or *blitzkrieg*, upon Norway. Still Hitler had not stirred against the French and British forces arrayed along his western frontier, and the French had felt safe behind the massive fortifications of their Maginot Line.

Then, before dawn on 10 May, Hitler had struck, launching the full force of a *blitzkrieg* not against those concrete defences but against the small neutral states of Belgium and the Netherlands adjoining, so that he could then wheel southwards and take France on her undefended flank. The Nazi *Luftwaffe* bombarded these countries from the air and dropped parachute troops, then still a novelty in war. Another novelty the Germans had developed was the *panzer* division of fast-moving armoured vehicles.

The unfortunate Dutch and Belgians scarcely knew what had hit them. The French and British, hastily leaving their positions to go to their aid, were no better off. No army was yet equipped to fight the Germans in this new 1940 style. It took just five days to convince the French Prime Minister that the war was lost.

Churchill was of sterner stuff. In any case – to be fair to the French – the British could still take comfort from the sea that lay between them and the invincible Nazis. For the moment, however, even that sea posed a problem: the British Army was on the wrong side of it, fighting a desperate rearguard action in a hopeless situation. That army could do no more, for the time being, on the mainland of Europe. The German High Command was publicly boasting, 'The British Army is threatened with annihilation.' Somehow it must be rescued and brought back to Britain to fight another day. If not, Britain would *have* no army, and there would *be* no other day, and Hitler's dictatorship would be everywhere supreme.

With the collapse of resistance by the Dutch and Belgians and the slower crumbling of the French – who finally and formally surrendered five weeks later – the main British forces fell back on Dunkirk, a French sea-port close to the frontier with Belgium. There, in that last week of May, something like a third of a million soldiers – British, French and Belgian – were hemmed into an ever-diminishing area, pounded by artillery and bombed or machine-gunned by low-flying aircraft against which they had no defence. Huddled amid the sand-dunes and on the open beaches, the troops found just one cause to be thankful – the sand was so deep and soft that some of the bombs did not explode on impact.

How to get them out? That was the problem. The shattered harbour of Dunkirk would serve for a number of vessels but the majority of the troops, if they were to be evacuated at all, would

have to be embarked straight from the shore, where the shallowness of the water called for boats.

No navy could have supplied sufficient craft of that kind to transport so many men. But the Admiralty rose to the unique emergency. At Dover Admiral Sir B. H. Ramsay began collecting a miscellaneous fleet of all the vessels available, and 'Operation Dynamo' began on the night of 26 May with the bringing of the first troops across the narrow seas.

From then onwards, at first secretly, and then with spontaneous volunteering as the word ran round, the epic of Dunkirk took shape. Boatyards were ransacked for motor launches. Liners in harbour gave up their lifeboats. Thames tugs and lighters, sailing barges and pleasure-yachts, fishing-smacks and river-steamers – almost everything that would float joined that fantastic ferry-service, crossing and recrossing the North Sea, taking off load after load of human cargo under the relentless bombardment of the Germans.

Luckily the weather was fine and warm, the sea smooth. For the rest of the twentieth century, so long as anyone survives who went through that experience, or even waited breathlessly for the news of it, a calm hot May will be 'Dunkirk weather', a reminder of the miracle. Sometimes the exhausted soldiers had to wade out through the water up to their necks before they could reach the vessel and be hauled aboard.

It was, of course, a defeat and a disaster. The British lost all their transport, their heavy equipment, and a thousand guns. But the men themselves got away – including their French and Belgian comrades, more than 337,000 of them. By 3 June the beaches lay empty under the sun. Among the last to leave were two officers, Alexander and Montgomery, destined to become the outstanding British generals in the happier days to come.

'Mr Boswell – from Scotland!'

Young James Boswell, rising and dressing with his usual care in his lodgings in Downing Street, had no notion that this day, Monday, 16 May 1763, was to be perhaps the most momentous day in his life.

He had given some thought to his programme in advance. He would send a pair of breeches to be mended. He was expecting two young friends to breakfast – he would give them toast, rolls and butter, and try to keep his new resolution to be more serious and behave with dignity. Then he would write up his journal, which he had kept since leaving his Scottish home and coming to London just six months ago. Afterwards he would go round and see James Love, the actor, who owed him forty pounds, and try to get some of it back. At the end of the day he was to visit Dr Pringle, a friend of his father's.

One way and another, the time should pass quite pleasantly.

At twenty-two, Boswell had still not settled on a career. He was considering a commission in the Guards, if he could get one, or becoming a lawyer like his father and grandfather before him. For the moment he was thoroughly enjoying the gay life of a man-about-town. Compared with the dour, decent Scotland he had fled from, the London of George III, with its playhouses and pleasure gardens, its girls and its gambling, offered a world of thrilling wickedness.

The day went very much to plan, save that he could extract only one miserable guinea from the actor. Then he went on to drink tea with another actor, Thomas Davies, who also kept a bookshop in Covent Garden.

It was there, at seven o'clock in the evening, that something occurred which had formed no part of his programme. The great Mr Samuel Johnson came in.

Johnson had still to be made 'Doctor' by his old university, but that he was already 'great' could be denied by nobody.

He had produced the famous dictionary. He was renowned as a writer of poetry and prose, a literary critic, and – above all, some would have said – a superb talker, throwing out in impromptu argument, gems of wit and wisdom that it was tragic not to have preserved on paper.

From his house in a quiet courtyard off Fleet Street, Johnson reigned over the intellectual society of London like an emperor. Boswell had been longing to make his acquaintance.

Now, as the big, bear-like author entered the bookshop, the young Scotsman was seized with misgivings.

Johnson, at fifty-three, was 'a very big man', Boswell recorded in his journal, 'very slovenly in his dress', speaking 'with a most uncouth voice', afflicted with a nervous twitch, and altogether 'a man of a most dreadful appearance'.

It was not this which worried Boswell – it was the knowledge that Johnson did not like Scotsmen. To Davies he appealed in an agitated whisper, 'Don't tell where I come from!'

But Davies mischievously introduced him as 'Mr Boswell – from Scotland!'

Johnson stared. 'Indeed, Mr Johnson,' faltered Boswell, 'I come from Scotland, but I cannot help it.'

'Sir,' said Johnson, with that majestic manner which made his hearers forget the uncouth voice, 'that, I find, is what a very great many of your countrymen cannot help.'

He had a fixed opinion that all Scotsmen really wanted to get out of their own country and escape to the south. As he said on another occasion, 'The noblest prospect that a Scotsman ever sees is the road which leads him to England!'

It was not a promising start for Boswell. For a time he took a back seat and contented himself with listening to the great man's conversation with other people. But Boswell was never easy to squash – like a rubber ball he had a thick skin and soon bounced up again. He was determined to join in the discussion.

Johnson was grumbling that David Garrick, then the leading actor in London, had refused him a complimentary theatre ticket for a friend.

'Oh, sir,' Boswell broke in, 'I cannot think Mr Garrick would grudge such a trifle to *you*.'

Johnson turned and scowled at him. 'Sir,' he rumbled, 'I have known David Garrick longer than you have done, and I know no right you have to talk to me on the subject.'

One might have thought that Boswell would have crept away after that, and never wanted to see Johnson again. Instead, he remained till ten o'clock, drinking in every word that fell from his lips, and leaving reluctantly only because he was expected at Dr Pringle's.

Boswell knew that Johnson was very much more than a disagreeable old bear – and Johnson soon learned that Boswell was much more than a tiresome young puppy.

After one or two more encounters a remarkable friendship developed between them. From that first evening Boswell resolved to remember as much as he could of Johnson's brilliant talk and striking opinions. Over the years he noted them in writing, and after Johnson's death in 1784 he used them as the basis for his *Life of Samuel Johnson*, one of the greatest biographies in the English language.

So, unexpectedly, that evening in Davies' bookshop was a landmark in literary history.

May Day

Bishop Hugh Latimer was annoyed. And with good reason.

He had arrived in a certain town, as he complained some time afterwards to the boy king, Edward VI, expecting to preach to a large congregation. He had every right to expect it, for ever since his release from the Tower on Henry VIII's death he had been one of the most popular preachers in the country, sure of packed churches wherever he mounted the pulpit. His sermons – homely, humorous, sometimes racy, often outspoken – played a great part, as is now realized, in promoting the Reformation in Tudor England.

On that particular day, however, things were very different.

The church door was locked and there was no sign of parson or congregation. Latimer waited for some time. At last a man appeared.

'Sir,' he said, 'this is a busy day with us. We cannot hear you. It is Robin Hood's day.'

Latimer could only accept the situation as philosophically as possible. The bishop's rochet – his long surplice-like vestment – 'was fain to give place to Robin Hood's men', he told King Edward when relating his experience.

By an unfortunate slip his visit had been booked for 1 May –

'May Day' or, as the parishioner had called it, 'Robin Hood's Day'.

May Day had been a great popular festival for centuries and for many years it had been specially connected with Robin Hood. Plays were acted in which he, and Maid Marian, and the other outlaws, re-enacted their adventures. In the household accounts of the Earl of Northumberland there is an item for providing 'liveries for Robin Hood', and in the *Paston Letters*, under the date 1473, Sir John laments the departure of a keeper whom he employed chiefly because he was so good at acting the parts of Robin and the Sheriff of Nottingham.

Everyone, high and low, was involved in these celebrations. One year the young King Henry VIII rode out 'a-maying' with his first wife, Catherine of Aragon, from their palace at Greenwich, and on Shooter's Hill 'they espied a company of tall yeomen, clothed all in green, with green hoods, and bows and arrows, to the number of two hundred'. Their leader saluted the King, announced himself as Robin Hood, and gave a signal by whistle, whereupon the whole band of archers loosed their shafts into the

air together, 'so that the noise was strange and loud, which greatly delighted the King, Queen, and their company'. After more displays of bowmanship, the royal party were invited into the neighbouring woodland, where they found arbours made of boughs and decked with spring flowers, and a plentiful spread of wine and venison 'to their great contentment'.

But Robin Hood was only one element in the day's celebrations, which included morris dancing, a maypole, and bonfires in the streets. That morning, wrote the Elizabethan historian, John Stow, 'every man, except impediment, would walk into the sweet meadows and green woods, there to rejoice their spirits with the beauty and savour of sweet flowers, and with the harmony of birds, praising God in their kind'.

Sometimes the festivities became livelier than most people intended. In 1517 May Day in London ended with a riot when the city youths set upon all the foreigners they met. After that, the authorities went a little easy on official celebrations of the festival, but in general May Day continued to be popular until the Puritans suppressed it, with so many other forms of fun, in the period of the Commonwealth. Even then, no sooner was Cromwell dead and Charles II on his way home, than up went the maypoles again.

But the spirit of the festival was never fully recaptured. It died with the coming of the Industrial Revolution, and what we see today – morris dancers and schoolgirl May Queens and so forth – is no more than a pretty and picturesque modern revival, a shadow of the old lusty, full-blooded national holiday, when even a famous bishop could be forgotten and locked out of the church.

May Day has acquired another, quite different, significance as an international day to be celebrated with processions and political demonstrations by Communists, Socialists and trade unionists. In Britain, though, this is observed with much less support than in China, Russia and many other countries, and the programme is usually postponed until the weekend. Only once has this British May Day had any notable historic connection –

in 1926, when it fell on the eve of the unsuccessful General Strike which for the next few days paralysed normal life throughout the country.

The Red Dragon Wakes

On 10 May 1404, a tall man in his mid-forties, with a forked beard and a weather-beaten face etched with lines of care, sat in the castle of Harlech on the Welsh coast composing a letter to the King of France.

He wrote persuasively, because he wanted help. But he wrote proudly, as to an equal. He signed himself *Owynus Dei Gratia Princeps Wallie*, 'Owen, by the grace of God, Prince of Wales', a title to which he felt he had more right than the son of any English king. He was the man Shakespeare called 'the great magician, damn'd Glendower', because his cunning as a guerrilla general, suddenly appearing and disappearing amid the misty hills, so often proved too much for the heavily armoured English knights who plodded in pursuit.

When he had signed the letter he pressed the soft wax with the splendid seal he had had made in his own likeness. One side showed him mounted, sword in hand. On the other he sat enthroned, holding orb and sceptre.

His envoys took the letter to King Charles, who welcomed them, gave them rich presents to take back, and promised to make a compact with 'the magnificent and mighty Owen, Prince of Wales'.

The French king suffered from frequent bouts of insanity, but his advisers were sane enough. In 1404, with France and England at enmity, an alliance with the Welsh rebels made good sense.

For more than a century Wales had been a conquered territory, held down by strong fortresses planted at key points by Edward I. Now, in the person of Owen Glendower, the red dragon was astir again and the Welsh people had liberated their country.

Sitting in Harlech Castle, one of the many places he had recaptured from their English garrisons, Glendower had a moment's leisure to look back along the hard road he had travelled in the past three or four years.

Though he had known from boyhood that the blood of the ancient Welsh princes flowed in his veins, from both sides of his family, he had begun by accepting the state of affairs as he found it. He had studied law at Oxford and the Inns of Court in London, he had served as squire to the English Earl of Arundel, and after marriage he had settled down as a loyal subject of the English crown. For four of his five daughters he was to choose English husbands.

His great fortified manor-house at Sycharth, in the Berwyn Hills, had been a happy place, full of life and merriment. Wandering bards were always welcome there. When the feasting was done, the harp-strings were plucked, and the age-old legends – along with the more recent historical adventures of warriors like Llewelyn the Great – were retold to thrill the listeners.

Yes, Sycharth had been a happy place in those days. Five boys, five girls, the stables full of wiry ponies, the hall full of hunting dogs . . . Always plenty to eat and drink – beef, mutton, venison, game, pigeons from the pigeon-house, rabbits from the warren, fish from the pond . . . Sycharth had everything. Orchards, even a vineyard.

A man could have been happy there all his life.

That blissful existence ended in 1400, when a jealous English neighbour, Lord Grey, persuaded King Henry IV that Glendower was disloyal. Grey got permission to seize his estates. He made a surprise raid upon Sycharth, and Glendower escaped only by taking to the woods.

So, almost by accident, he was forced into becoming a rebel. And the wild enthusiasm with which people rallied to help him, his pride in Wales, and his knowledge that Henry himself was no more than a usurper, who had just deposed and probably murdered Richard II – all these factors combined to push him along the road.

His followers hailed him as Prince of Wales. He accepted the title and hoisted his Red Dragon standard on the summit of Plynlimmon. Throughout 1401 he swept triumphantly across South Wales.

Early in 1402 a bright comet was seen, red, fiery and dragon-like. One of the bards, Red Iolo, hailed it as a sign of victory. And that year was indeed a year of victories. Castle after castle fell into Welsh hands. When English expeditions were sent into the mountains, they were frustrated by the wildness of the country and its weather, and by the brilliant guerrilla tactics with which Glendower's forces harassed them.

He was much more than a guerrilla leader, however. He was a diplomat, an astute politician. He knew that Wales could not for ever stand against the might of a united England. So England must be split – and why not, when many Englishmen still re-garded Henry as a usurper? Glendower made a pact with Harry Percy (Shakespeare's Hotspur) and with Mortimer, that they should divide England, north and south, between them and leave him in control of Wales.

Glendower dreamed of a completely independent Wales. He called a Welsh parliament and planned to establish two uni-versities.

For several years that dream had a chance of being realized. True, Prince Hal, the future Henry V, managed to burn down beautiful Sycharth and Glendower's other country home, but such revengeful gestures were petty compared with Glendower's triumphs. The French alliance brought a fleet and an army, with which the Welsh invaded England almost as far as Worcester. But by then, 1405, the tide was beginning to turn. Glendower had shot his bolt.

In 1409 Harlech Castle, from which he had written so proudly to France, was recaptured by the English. Glendower's wife, two of his daughters, and three of his grandchildren were taken prisoner and carried off as hostages to the Tower of London.

Glendower himself was never caught. He ended his days as a shadowy outlaw, possibly under the protection of another daughter, Alice Scudamore, in Herefordshire. He is believed to have died about 1415 and to have been buried in that county at Monington.

A Horse for a Hostage

How to escape?

That was the thought uppermost in the Lord Edward's mind throughout the month of May 1265.

He and his father, King Henry III, were no better than prisoners in their own castle at Hereford. It had been so for a whole year since, on 14 May 1264, they had lost the Battle of Lewes to the rebellious barons under the great Earl of Leicester, Simon de Montfort. Edward had not been captured in the fight, but he had surrendered two days afterwards as a hostage.

Since then, Simon had been the real ruler of England. The King had been forced to go with him everywhere and do as Simon told him.

Henry, son of King John, who had also faced trouble with his barons and had granted Magna Carta almost fifty years earlier, was a weak character, no match for the iron-hard Simon. Men called him 'Heart of Wax'.

Edward was quite different. His nickname was 'Longshanks'. He was tall and athletic, a handsome tawny-haired Plantagenet prince of twenty-five, fearless in battle and as hard as Simon. He chafed at captivity. His blood boiled to see his royal father so meek and helpless.

It did not help matters that Simon was his uncle – the Earl had married the King's sister. So the King was the prisoner of his own brother-in-law, and Edward's own particular guard was his cousin, young Henry de Montfort, one of the Earl's sons. When Simon found it necessary to march his army into South Wales, he took the King with him but left Edward at Hereford under the watchful eye of his son.

It was, of course, impossible to keep Edward chained in a dungeon. Like the King, he had to be treated with every outward sign of respect. It would never have done for the common people to understand who was really running the country. But Edward knew well enough that he was watched day and night, and that, while he could walk about the castle and even go riding, he was not free to leave Hereford. In any case, until he had friends powerful enough to stand up to the de Montfort party, where could he possibly go?

He knew that disagreements had broken out between his uncle and some of his former allies, men like Roger Mortimer, one of the Marcher Lords holding sway in that hilly border country of the Welsh Marches, and Gilbert de Clare, Earl of Gloucester. Gilbert's brother, Thomas de Clare, still seemed faithful to the de Montforts. He remained in Hereford and was one of the men guarding Edward.

Thomas de Clare, nonetheless, proved to be the answer to Edward's problem. By cautious probings Edward found that Thomas was in touch with his brother and ready to change sides.

So at Whitsuntide, late in May, a plan of escape was worked out. No record exists of the precise details. There are, as the modern newspapers say, 'conflicting accounts'. As there were not even newspapers in 1265, let alone books of memoirs and autobiographies, it is not surprising that in later years the story varied in the telling.

The most ingenious version is that a new horse was sent as a present to Edward and that, wanting naturally to try its paces, he rode out with his escort into the great common meadow, known as Widemarsh, which lay just outside the town walls.

There he challenged Henry de Montfort and the others to a race. When he sighted, in the distance, a group of armed riders clustered on a hill, and knew them to be friends, he wheeled his horse and made a dash in their direction, closely followed by Thomas de Clare.

Other accounts simply say that he gave his captors the slip while hunting. What is certain is that a horse played a vital part in his escape. Once he had shaken off his pursuers, he rode northwards up the old Roman road to Mortimer's safe stronghold at Wigmore.

Henry de Montfort had the unpleasant task of informing his father, on campaign in Wales, that the heir to the throne was free and rallying all the forces opposed to Simon's government.

It had been an expensive mistake. A little more than two months later, on 4 August, Simon's army was trapped in the horseshoe curve of the Severn at Evesham by Edward and his allies, Roger Mortimer and the de Clares. The result was a massacre. The Earl fell and was almost hacked to pieces. Many of his followers drowned in the river as they tried to flee. The King was lucky to be rescued alive – he had been taken into the middle of the army by his captors and would have been cut down if he had not identified himself in time, calling out: 'I am Henry of Winchester! Your King!' That was the end of the Barons' War. Thereafter, Edward supplied the strong guiding hand his father needed, and in 1272 he became king as Edward I.

June

Midsummer Night Watch

Throughout most of British history, from Stonehenge down to Stuart times, Midsummer Day (24 June) and the preceding night were a landmark in the year which people loved to celebrate. The Christian Church helped by its usual practice of taking over an ancient pagan festival and turning it into a saint's day – 24 June became John the Baptist's – but the old superstitions lingered in people's minds. Midsummer Night, as Shakespeare's comedy reminds us, was the time when fairies and mischievous spirits like Puck were at large.

That play also reminds us that it was the night when the woods were full of wandering mortals too, young lovers snatching a few hours together and amateur actors, like Bottom and his friends, preparing their entertainment for the following day.

Shakespeare was reflecting the customs of Tudor England. One practice was to go out into the woods and cut green branches, bringing them home to fasten over the doors in honour of St John. The boys and girls, the real-life Lysanders and Demetriuses, the Hermias and Helenas, probably thought it as good an excuse as any to slip away from their elders into the midnight darkness of the trees – and if eerie noises startled them suddenly with thoughts of hobgoblins, it was an excellent reason for holding hands and clinging together for reassurance.

Most of the fathers and elder brothers were fully occupied elsewhere. One of the most popular customs was the great parade known as the Midsummer Night Watch, though Shakespeare does not introduce it into his play, probably because it had been given up in London in Henry VIII's time on the score of expense.

In smaller towns it continued. Nottingham kept the practice until Charles I's reign.

All the citizens paraded at sunset on Midsummer Eve and took an oath to keep the peace. They carried what arms they possessed, so that the parade served as a muster of able-bodied men who could be relied on in an emergency, but they wore garlands because it was a festive occasion. It was because of this that the affair had got out of hand in wealthy London – there had been such lavish spending on gilded armour, scarlet cloaks and so forth, every one trying to outdo his neighbour by hiring torch-bearers and trumpeters and great horses – but in other places the men simply turned out in the best they had.

After taking the oath, they formed parties to patrol the streets during the short summer night, with frequent pauses for rest and refreshment. The women looked down from their bedroom windows, bandying jokes and gossip with the men below, though we may guess that many ran downstairs and opened the front door, if only to offer cakes and ale.

Provided that it did not rain, a good time was had by all. And when the early sun came up over the gabled roofs, and people suddenly remembered the younger generation and wondered why their beds had not been slept in, either, the lads and lasses had their explanation pat.

'We went to the woods,' they said, adding with an innocent expression, '*someone* had to cut the branches to go over the door, and everyone else seemed so busy.' And they held up the leafy boughs in justification.

D Day: The Way Back

Just four years after the British Army had been driven out of France by Hitler, they went back.

The Dunkirk evacuation had ended on 3 June 1940, though for some weeks afterwards there had been considerable other British forces making their escape through the more westerly French ports. Then, for four grim years, the fighting had raged elsewhere, in Russia and North Africa, Greece and Sicily, the Far East, the sea, and the skies above the industrial cities of Britain and Germany.

France was occupied and held down by her Nazi conquerors. There was much underground 'resistance', much passing of spies and saboteurs to and fro across the Channel, but apart from one or two daring commando raids of a hit-and-run type it was not until 6 June 1944 that the British could go back in strength, openly, and prepared to stay.

If Dunkirk had been a miracle of make-shift, D Day was a masterpiece of planning and preparation. The very phrase, 'D Day', illustrates this.

The invasion called for the most precise timing. One advance unit, for example, might be required to take a certain action or reach a certain objective on the first day. Another kind of unit, with some sort of auxiliary role, might not be required until forty-eight hours later – and would upset the programme if it moved too soon. Yet, with the weather at sea unpredictable, it was impossible to fix an exact date beforehand – the planners could only say that, because of the tides and the phases of the moon, a few days in each month were suitable. So, as the sealed plans accumulated, with all the detailed instructions in a carefully worked-out time sequence, it was not possible to speak of '5 June' and '7 June' and the days were indicated as 'D Day' and 'D plus 2' respectively.

This was just as well. For when 5 June came, the weather in the Channel was too rough. General Eisenhower, the American in supreme command of the operation, had to postpone it for twenty-four hours, and 'D Day' became 6 June.

For months beforehand the invasion armies had been mustering in camps throughout southern England – Americans, British, Canadians, Free French, and others. This time the transport was not left to an improvised fleet of assorted vessels. There were 4,000 ships and innumerable smaller craft, including the oblong landing-craft that let down drawbridges in the bows so that tanks and men could pour straight out on to the beaches. The Americans had amphibious vehicles known as D.U.K.W.s. Overhead, the allies had immense air power to saturate the German positions with bombs and to clear the skies for the landing of troops by parachute and glider. In four years they had mastered Hitler's idea of the *blitzkrieg* and improved upon it.

The Germans, on the other hand, had repeated the mistake of the French in 1940, over the Maginot Line, and had put their faith in the Atlantic Wall, a fortification system girdling the French coast. They could not imagine how an attack from the sea could pierce it. They reckoned, too, that a big invading force could not succeed unless it had the use of a harbour to bring in heavy equipment and supplies. They made sure that all the French ports were impregnable.

The invaders had foreseen that difficulty and taken steps. In complete secrecy they had designed and built two artificial 'harbours' in a number of prefabricated sections. As soon as the first troops were safely ashore and had established a beachhead, these 'Mulberry Harbours' were towed across the Channel and fitted together to make long jetties and breakwaters, providing calm water and the same unloading facilities as a port.

Oil – so vital for keeping a mechanized army in action – did not need to be unloaded at all. Yet another of the well-kept D Day secrets was 'Pluto', a pipe-line swiftly laid across the sea-floor of the Channel, enabling oil to be pumped straight from the Isle of Wight to Normandy.

It was the minute attention given to this and a thousand other problems, small and great, that enabled 'Operation Overlord' to succeed. There was, of course, fierce fighting. The mined beaches and the fire-power of the German defenders took a heavy toll of the attackers as they waded ashore, yet, considering the scale of the battle, the historians have called the casualties 'remarkably small'.

By 'D plus 5' – 11 June – the British and American forces, led by Montgomery, had captured fifty miles of the Normandy coast and pushed ten or fifteen miles inland.

Plenty of tough warfare lay ahead. It was to take another eleven months before Montgomery accepted the surrender of all the German armies in the West, and Eisenhower, two days afterwards, the surrender of Germany as a whole.

But D Day began the process of victory and liberation. On that day the British won their way back into the Europe from which they had been driven in the perilous summer of 1940.

The Long Ships Come to Lindisfarne

On 8 June 793, the Vikings suddenly appeared in their long ships, with their terrifying dragon prows, off the peaceful Northumbrian islet of Lindisfarne.

It was just because the spot was so peaceful and remote from the outside world – an island three miles long and less than two miles wide, cut off from the mainland at high water – that St

Aidan and his Irish monks had come there a century and a half earlier and founded the monastery which earned the place the other name of Holy Island, and the description, 'cradle of English Christianity'.

The monks and hermits loved such islands. All round the coasts of the British Isles, the wilder and lonelier the better, they chose them as refuges. They were wise to do so in the Dark Ages, when the mainland of Europe was overrun by the heathen barbarians who had destroyed the Roman Empire. Such island sanctuaries did much to preserve Christianity and civilization.

Unfortunately, a new enemy appeared against whom rough seas and rocks were no protection. The Vikings liked islands too. They could land on them and plunder freely, with no fear that help would arrive to the rescue of their victims. And a monastery was a fine place to loot, being well provided with gold and silver vessels and candle-sticks, precious jewelled crucifixes and relics, and rare cloths, in the shape of robes and vestments and altar hangings.

Lindisfarne was one of the very richest of such island monasteries and its fame was all too well known. It was the first to be sacked by the Vikings. It was not the last.

A Durham monk, Simeon, described that day. Writing centuries later, he recorded how the heathen pirates 'laid everything waste, with grievous plundering. They trampled the sacred places with unclean steps, dug up the altars and laid hands on all the treasures. Some of the monks they slew, others they carried off in chains, many they cast out, some they threw into the sea.'

Lindisfarne was left a ruin. It was rebuilt, but when the Vikings came raiding again, many years later, the monks abandoned the island as too exposed. They took with them the body of their one-time prior, St Cuthbert, and finally found refuge in Durham.

To get a faint idea of the beauty and civilization that once flourished in the holy island before the Vikings came, one has only to visit the British Museum and look at the 'Lindisfarne Gospels', the book once lovingly written and illustrated in the cloister there as a memorial to St Cuthbert.

In it are the Gospels in Latin, with a Saxon translation written between the lines, centuries later, by a priest named Aldred. A hermit, Bifrith, who was a skilful artist, contributed portraits of each evangelist to the Gospel bearing his name, and illuminated the elaborate capital letters at the beginning of each section. Some other craftsman, at the bishop's order, made a binding for the volume of gold set with precious stones. Perhaps only the rather similar Book of Kells, preserved in Dublin, can match its beauty.

The King at Bay

The first thing one asks oneself is, why did they have to meet in an open meadow beside the Thames? Why not in some great castle hall or the chapter-house of an abbey? True, they fixed the meeting for 15 June, but an English June could bring just as vile weather in 1215 as it can today.

The obvious answer is that neither side trusted the other. If they had gathered at Windsor Castle, a few miles away, the barons would have felt they were entering the lion's den. In London, on the other hand, King John would have been at the mercy of the citizens, who were making common cause with the rebellious noblemen.

So they agreed on a flat field at Runnymede, between Staines and Windsor. Then there could be no ambush, no scope for treachery, and every one would be free to ride away if they could not come to an agreement.

John knew in his heart that there would have to be an agreement. He was at bay. For years he had ruled his kingdom with difficulty, making enemies on all sides and rousing them to the threat of open rebellion. Now they all seemed to be united against him – the powerful lords, the bishops and clergy, the merchants of London and the smaller cities.

He was angry and desperate as he rode into the meadow. He was a strongly-built, burly man, five feet six in height (as we know from his skeleton), not tall by modern standards but a fair height for the Middle Ages. He was going bald, but the curly long hair that remained was reddish and, combined with his small beard, gave him a foxy look which matched his crafty character.

He loved fine clothes and was notorious for the money he spent on them. His effigy in Worcester Cathedral shows him wearing a gold-edged tunic of crimson silk, a mantle and under-tunic of cloth-of-gold, red hose, black shoes with golden spurs, white gloves and a jewelled belt. When the tomb beneath was opened in 1797, his bones were still clad in the tattered remnants of these very garments.

At Runnymede he put on the best show he could. In his party were the Archbishop of Canterbury and a group of other bishops, Pandulf, the Pope's representative in England, William Marshal, Earl of Pembroke, and other leading earls and barons. But John knew well that many of these men followed him only as a formal duty. Many, including the Archbishop, were as firm in opposition to him as the formidable crowd of noblemen he could see massed against him on the other side of the field.

The conference took some time, for there were many points to settle. The barons wanted firm, unbreakable promises from the King, set out in a charter bearing his seal. Mainly, as big landowners, they were out to safeguard the interests of their own class and to limit the King's power over them. But they needed the backing of the Archbishop and the Church, so they had to include demands for their benefit too. Similarly, they must not forget the townsmen whose money was so useful.

In the end the charter, the Great Charter or Magna Carta, to give it its Latin name, took more than a week to draft and ran to dozens of clauses. From that first day, Monday, 15 June, until Tuesday week, 23 June, the King had to ride out every morning from Windsor to take part in the discussions.

It took time, dealing with all those clauses and wording them so that the most cunning ruler could not wriggle out of his bargain. The men who drafted the charter knew that they were doing something important, but they did not realize how important, or that Magna Carta would be remembered more than seven hundred years later and regarded (not always quite accurately) as the foundation-stone of British liberty.

At last the work was finished. Numerous copies had to be

made, each diligently written out in ink on parchment rolls, to be sent out all over the kingdom with open letters, or 'letters patent', from the King to his sheriffs, so that the conditions of the charter should be made known to all.

John did not actually 'sign' the document by writing his name, but he sealed it. Four copies bearing his Great Seal are still in existence, two of them in the British Museum, the others belonging to the cathedrals of Lincoln and Salisbury. There are several other copies without his seal.

That night, back in Windsor Castle, John tossed and turned, unable to sleep. Now that the conference was over not only the barons but his own Council had departed, and in the words of the chronicler, Roger of Wendover, writing at the time, he 'was left with scarcely seven knights out of his proper body of attendants'. For the moment he was helpless. But he could think of nothing but revenge and how, by hook or by crook, he could upset the agreement.

The next morning, stealthily, he took horse and set off for the comparative safety of the Isle of Wight. There his plans began to take shape. Pandulf, the Pope's representative, was despatched to Rome with those promises that persuaded Innocent III, on 24 August, to declare the charter null and void. Other messengers crossed the Channel to the King's overseas possessions, to muster troops for a counter move.

John did not live long enough, however, to undo the work done in those June days at Runnymede. Just over a year later, in October 1216, he died at Newark.

A New Day Dawns for Victoria

Sunrise is early on 20 June, for the next day is the longest in the year. But on that date in 1837 the dawn was only just breaking when a carriage drove out through the gates of Windsor Castle and took the road to London more than twenty miles away. Two sombre figures sat within the carriage. One was the Archbishop of Canterbury, the other the Lord Chamberlain.

It was broad daylight, with the birds singing, when they reached Kensington, then still a pleasant countrified suburb. The carriage stopped in front of the Palace and the two gentlemen got out, nerving themselves for the scene that lay ahead. Though the birds were awake, nobody in the Palace seemed to be. It was only after long and thunderous knocking – rather an undignified anti-climax for such a momentous occasion – that the door was opened by a bleary-eyed servant. It was just five o'clock.

It was about six when the Princess Victoria was awakened by her mother, twittering with excitement. They still shared the same bedroom as they had always done, though Victoria was now eighteen. This was not from necessity – they had ample accommodation in the Palace and King William had just given his niece an allowance of £10,000 a year, quite independent of her mother, the Duchess of Kent. But the Duchess, a former German princess, jealous of her rights and most tactless in asserting them, did not intend the girl to be independent. She meant to keep her under her thumb – and Victoria's meek daughterly demeanour made her think it would be easy.

Victoria was not surprised by the news her mother broke to

her. Her uncle had been ill, she knew that he had been sinking during the past day or two. Now he had died in the night and they had come to tell her that she was Queen of England.

She was prepared for this moment. She had prayed and thought about it a good deal. A serious girl, despite her love of dancing and riding and other amusements, she was old enough to understand the responsibility that had fallen upon her shoulders. Nothing in her life would ever be the same again.

Her mother, always at odds with the King, made little effort to hide her pleasure or to pretend a sorrow she did not feel. But Victoria thought kindly of the odd, outspoken old sailor who had gone. In different circumstances uncle and niece could have got on well together. The Duchess had stopped that.

The Archbishop and Lord Conyngham were waiting. The girl

did not delay. Calmly she put on her dressing-gown and went through into her sitting-room to receive them. If her mother had expected to go with her, she was disappointed. Victoria was now something else besides a daughter. She was a queen. '*Alone*', she wrote in her journal when she entered up the doings of that historic day. She underlined the word.

Alone she stood in her dressing-gown as the Lord Chamberlain went down on one knee and told her officially that King William IV was dead. Alone, at nine o'clock, in plain black, she welcomed the Prime Minister, Lord Melbourne, resplendent in his court dress. Alone, at half-past eleven, she held her first Council in the red saloon. Her dignity astonished the eminent statesmen and officers assembled there. 'She not only filled her chair, she filled the room,' said the Duke of Wellington afterwards.

So began that extraordinary reign of sixty-three years, during which Britain attained her highest point as a world power and Victoria herself became a living legend.

It was busy, that first day which had begun so early. There were important people to receive, letters to write, decisions to make, orders to give.

One order concerned a purely personal matter, but it had its deep historical significance. She wished her bed to be taken out of her mother's room. From now onwards she would sleep *alone*.

Highway Robbery

It was a hot day on 23 June 1652. Otherwise, young John Evelyn would not have made the mistake of riding so close to the hedge-row to enjoy the shade.

He had made another mistake, by sending his man ahead of him. He was quite alone, travelling from Tunbridge Wells towards the home he hoped to enjoy in peace and quiet, now that Oliver Cromwell's recent victories had put an end to the Civil War. Everything was going well. He was thirty-one and in good health. His young wife had just arrived safely from Paris without misadventure, despite the perilous conditions in the English Channel. In a month or two she was to bear him a child. He had left her to rest in safety with her mother at Tunbridge Wells and was preceding them to make sure that the house at Deptford was all ready to welcome them.

It was a wonderful spring and summer that year. It had scarcely rained for four months past. It was little wonder that Evelyn, sweltering in the heavy clothes of a seventeenth-century gentle-man, sought what shelter he could find from the sun.

He was within three miles of Bromley when two villainous footpads leapt from the shadows, seized his reins and pulled him from the saddle. There was no chance to draw his sword. He was dragged some distance into a dense thicket, disarmed, and his riding boots pulled off. Then his hands were tied behind his back, and his legs bound, and he was propped helpless like a bundle against the trunk of an oak.

If he made a sound, they promised him with blood-curdling oaths, they would cut his throat. With deft fingers they went through his belongings. He had not much money with him, but they seized on a pair of valuable buckles, set with diamonds and rubies, and his two rings, one having an emerald and diamonds, the other an onyx. He asked to keep the latter, pointing out that it was engraved with his arms and would give them away, but they were not persuaded.

They took his silver-hilted sword and other trifles, and removed the horse's saddle, searching it for hidden valuables but in vain. Then, leaving the saddle on the ground and the horse tethered to a tree – they dared not take the beast, Evelyn knew, because it was cropped on both ears and its ownership well known in the district – they walked back to their prisoner and threatened him with their cocked pistols.

He had better keep quiet, they warned him, for they would not be far away. They had not meant to stop him, it was a richer prize they were expecting. They were a gang of fourteen altogether, and they had long guns as well as the pistols and iron staves he had seen. With that, the couple vanished through the undergrowth.

Evelyn was sceptical about their story of a dozen accomplices and felt pretty sure that they would not linger in the neighbourhood, but in that solitary spot, some distance from the highway, he might have called for hours without being heard. He himself could hear nothing but the sound of his own horse grazing, some sheep that were similarly engaged, and the buzzing flies which, along with ants and the hot sun slanting on his face, tormented him in his helplessness. He wondered anxiously how long he would have to spend there.

For nearly two hours he wrestled desperately with the cords around his wrists. His hands were bound back to back. At last he managed to turn them palm to palm. Then he was able to edge the cord down to his thumbs and, with more persistence, wriggle them under. The cord slackened and fell free. Then it did not take him long to unbind his feet, saddle his horse, and find his way back to the road.

A mild man by nature, Evelyn was now thirsting for revenge

– or justice at least. He rode at once to a magistrate, Colonel Blount, who sent out the hue and cry, the ancient order under which the law-abiding people in each parish were commanded to arrest any escaping felons within their own boundaries.

The next morning, still sore from his bonds, Evelyn rode to London, got five hundred leaflets printed, and arranged for their distribution. Within two days he got news of all the stolen items except the sword and a few trifles. One ring had been accepted at a pawnshop before the pawnbroker received the leaflet. The other had been bought, in all innocence, by a victualler who was then arrested when he tried to re-sell it to a goldsmith. So Evelyn regained most of his property, though in this case the thieves escaped unpunished.

How common highway robbery was, in the seventeenth century, is shown by the fact that Evelyn's friend, the other great diarist, Samuel Pepys, was robbed by two masked men when driving in his coach to Chelsea in 1693. In this case the highwaymen were afterwards identified and Pepys gave evidence against them at the Old Bailey, after which both men were sentenced to death.

July

The Fourth of July

Americans all over the world celebrate the Fourth of July as the most important date in their national history. It is a key date in British history too. It is the date on which Britain lost an empire she might, by more wisdom, have kept a good deal longer, though not for ever. But it is not an unhappy or shameful anniversary even for the British. For, in losing their American colonies, they learned a lesson which helped them, later on, to behave more sensibly towards Canada, Australia, New Zealand, and other nations that developed within the Empire.

What, exactly, happened on 4 July 1776? And first, what had led up to that historic day?

For more than a century and a half the English had been sailing across the Atlantic to establish settlements on the east coast of what is now the United States. John Smith founded Virginia in 1608. The Pilgrim Fathers sailed in the *Mayflower*, in 1620, seeking freedom for their strict Puritan way of life: from their small beginning developed the five separate colonies making up New England. Roman Catholics, also seeking freedom to worship in their own way, founded Maryland in 1633. North Carolina was largely started by French Huguenots, South Carolina by Ulster Presbyterians. Both colonies were named after Charles II. It was in his reign, too, that New York, New Jersey and Delaware were taken from the Dutch, and that the Quakers colonized Pennsylvania.

So, by the time of George III, there were thirteen separate colonies strung along the Atlantic coast of North America. They were made up of very different types of people, but, as the years went by, they came to realize that they had one thing in common: a dislike of being governed from London – thousands of miles and several weeks of sailing time distant – when they were not allowed to send representatives to Parliament and have any say in what was decided there.

Most of all, they objected to paying taxes to this remote government. They remembered that the English themselves had fought and beaten King Charles I in a civil war to make sure that they should pay only taxes voted by Parliament. What was right for the English in the 1640s was surely right for the American colonists in the 1770s? 'No taxation without representation,' they said. The colonies had their own elected assemblies, it is true, but their governors were appointed in England, and the colonies had no power to alter the trade regulations imposed by London, a scheme of duties and restrictions which had the effect of crippling American trade.

The Americans protested – respectfully, repeatedly, but with gradually mounting anger. Many individual Englishmen sympathized with them, but the government of George III maintained a stiff-necked attitude. In those days children were considered as

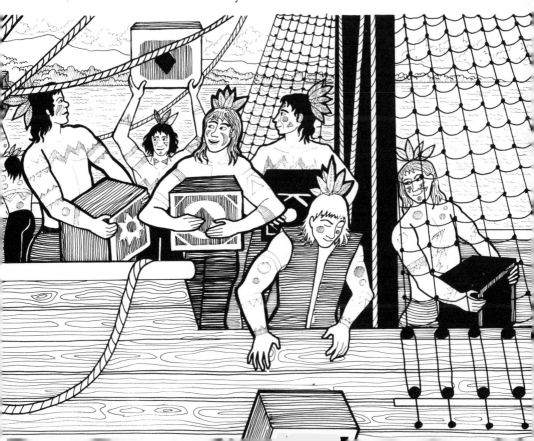

existing for the benefit of their parents: so too colonies existed for the benefit of the mother-country. They were not encouraged to grow up and demand rights of their own.

As early as 1770 British troops were forced to open fire on violent demonstrators in Boston. In 1773 came the famous 'Boston Tea Party'. The people were indignant at having to pay duty on tea. When an East Indiaman docked in Boston with her cargo of tea, a crowd of young men disguised themselves as Red Indian warriors in feathers and war-paint, raided the vessel, and tipped all the tea-chests overboard.

The British Parliament responded with acts of repression. Boston harbour was closed, the Massachusetts Assembly was suspended, and a soldier, General Gage, was sent out to govern the colony. The trial of Boston rioters was taken out of the hands of the local courts and referred to England.

Although the different colonies by no means agreed on everything they saw now that there was a threat to all of them. They decided to forget their own rivalries and quarrels for the time being, and send delegates to a meeting which they called the 'Continental Congress' to discuss how best they could act together.

This meeting was held at Philadelphia, the capital of Pennsylvania, at this time the biggest city in any of the colonies, with 40,000 inhabitants.

At this stage few Americans wanted independence. They merely wanted justice and a proper say in their own affairs. They were determined not to be bullied by London and cowed by the muskets of the redcoats. General Gage, for his part, was resolute to do his duty and maintain the authority of King George.

The first armed clash was at Lexington in April 1775. The colonists began to enrol in the ranks of their own militia. A second Continental Congress voted to appoint a Virginian planter, George Washington, commander-in-chief. Before he could reach the camp of the colonial forces, there had been a second battle, at Bunker Hill, won by the British but only with heavy casualties. The War of American Independence – as it was later called – had now really started.

The Declaration of Independence did not come for another year. Again the Continental Congress assembled in the elegant State House at Philadelphia. John Trumbull's famous painting, now hung in the Capitol, shows the delegates in their knee-breeches and stockings, ranged in the hall with crossed banners on the wall and the presiding officers at a paper-strewn table on a low dais.

It was at this gathering that the colonists decided to cut loose from the mother-country and found the United States of America.

There is no very strong reason for choosing 4 July as the exact date to celebrate. The essential vote was taken on 2 July. Thomas Jefferson, another Virginian planter and later to become one of the most famous American presidents, was given the task of wording the Declaration. His draft was agreed to with very few alterations. Perhaps the sonorous phrases owe something to Welsh eloquence as well as to Jefferson's own intellectual and philosophic cast of mind, for his father had come from Glyn-ceiriog in North Wales.

'All men are created equal; they have a right to life, liberty and the pursuit of happiness . . .' With those words begins the famous document which was to inspire not only the American colonists in 1776 but countless other seekers after freedom in far-off countries at distant future dates.

They were read to Congress on 4 July, and adopted, only the New York delegates abstaining. New York's agreement was announced on 15 July, and on 19 July Congress ordered the Declaration to be 'engrossed' – that is, written out in legal form on parchment – and signed. So we cannot speak of its being 'signed' on 4 July. This was not done until 2 August, and at least six signatures were not added until later – one indeed, by Thomas McKean of Delaware, as late as 1781.

Those details do not matter. The Declaration had been made, and its effects were profound. The war dragged on for another five years. Washington's armies suffered many a setback and there were moments when it seemed as though the British redcoats, helped by German mercenaries, would destroy Jefferson's dreams of liberty. But it was not so, the tide turned, and two centuries later the people of the United States can celebrate the Fourth of July – while their British friends, with good-humour and without a lingering trace of rancour, can join with them in the festivities.

Plymouth Hoe

'We've time enough to finish the game – and beat the Spaniards too.'

Those words, spoken with Francis Drake's lazy West Country drawl, have come down the ages. They conjure up the scene of a summer's afternoon, the green turf of Plymouth Hoe, the smooth land-locked waters of the Sound, the forest of bare masts on the anchored fleet, and the cluster of sun-tanned captains in doublet and hose, intent on their bowls.

Did it happen? Were the words ever spoken? If so, was it dangerously slack of Drake to waste time on a game when the news had just arrived that the Spanish Armada had been sighted at last off the Isles of Scilly?

The story cannot be absolutely proved. Those were days when there were no pressmen, no television news cameras, recording every detail as it happened. But Drake's famous words were being quoted within the lifetime of many who fought the Armada, so there is good reason to accept them.

They fit the man, that dare-devil confident sea-dog who had sailed into Cadiz harbour to 'singe the King of Spain's beard' and whom Queen Elizabeth had knighted on the deck of his own *Golden Hind*, for being the first Englishman to sail round the world.

They fit the situation too. It was not affectation that impelled Drake to continue his game, it was his knowledge of local waters and sailing conditions. At that moment, about three o'clock on the afternoon of 19 July 1588, the tide was just beginning to flow into the Sound. With that current against them, and a south-westerly breeze in their faces as well, the English could not possibly put to sea. There was no point in fuss and flurry. It was better to keep up morale by seeming casual, whatever one's private thoughts.

Drake and his fellow captains knew what they were up against. King Philip of Spain was so sure of his triumph that he had published every detail of his fleet before it sailed. Printed copies had been on sale throughout Europe. Burghley, Queen Elizabeth's secretary, had the information, even to the exact number of cannon balls the Spanish expedition carried: 123,790.

Drake knew that 130 vessels of different types and sizes were now entering the English Channel. They came not only from Spanish ports but from Sicily, Naples, Genoa, Venice, even Ragusa. There were ten Portuguese galleons, accustomed to the Atlantic rollers. But it was comforting to remember that in all that host of shipping, spread over miles of sea, only about fifty pure warships were included. The rest were transports, packed with 20,000 of the finest soldiers in Europe, and a mass of stores and equipment.

Another 30,000 troops were waiting near Dunkirk, in the Spanish Netherlands. The Armada was to carry them across the narrow seas for the actual invasion of England.

England was nerving herself for that invasion. The Queen declared herself determined to lead her own people in defence of the realm. Warning beacons were piled ready on hilltops. Now they were lit. In a few hours the news had been flashed along the south coast to Dover and the English vessels patrolling off Dunkirk. Just as quickly, the warning went north up the backbone of England to the Scottish border.

Meanwhile, we may well believe that, if Drake was playing bowls at all, he had ample leisure to complete his game. It was after ten o'clock that night when, with the tide on the ebb to help them, the English fleet struggled out into the open sea where they could manœuvre.

Then, in the days that followed, came the long running dog-fight up the Channel, what Garrett Mattingly has called, in his book *The Defeat of the Spanish Armada*, 'the first modern naval battle in history'. After that, the raid with fire-ships which began the demoralization of the Spaniards at Calais. And then more fighting in the North Sea, and finally the storms that completed the disintegration of the Armada.

The summer of threatened invasion was over. Not till the time of Napoleon in 1804, and of Hitler in 1940, was England to face that sort of threat again.

The Bitter Memory of the Boyne

One of the anniversaries that would be better forgotten is 12 July, in view of the bitterness and even bloodshed it can still provoke after almost three centuries. But as it is also one of the best-remembered dates in history, at least among Irishmen wherever they are met together in any part of the world, it is as well that everyone should know, as calmly and unemotionally as possible, precisely what occurred on that day in 1690.

Eighteen months before, the Glorious Revolution had driven James II from England and replaced him on the throne with his daughter, Mary, and her Dutch husband, William of Orange. The conflict was – on the surface, at least – religious. Great Britain was predominantly Protestant, but Ireland was Roman Catholic except in the northeast, where it had been largely taken over by

English and Scottish settlers. So Catholic James naturally looked to the Irish to help him regain his kingdom.

Louis XIV of France, the most powerful monarch in Europe, was ready to assist. He lent fifteen warships and several thousand troops. With this backing, James landed in Ireland, entered Dublin in triumph, and marched northwards, gathering Irish supporters, to besiege the town of Derry, as Catholics resolutely call it to this day, though it was officially renamed 'Londonderry' in 1613 because of its connection with the English companies.

William sent troops to fight his father-in-law. They were at first commanded by a veteran French Protestant, Marshal Schomberg, and included other Huguenot exiles. So, in this curious and tragic campaign, there were not only Irishmen on both sides but Frenchmen too, not to mention Scots and English lined up according to their religious loyalties – and the seasoned Dutch troops sent by William. This seems less odd when one remembers that this was not a war for Ireland or even solely for Britain, but part of the much wider European struggle which was all that really interested the former Prince of Orange.

The siege of Derry dragged on but was raised at last by English warships. Operations in Ireland went too slowly for William's liking. He decided to go over and take command himself. He looked forward, he declared, to 'being on horseback and under canvas again'. He was thankful to leave the tedious political arguments in London to his obedient wife, Queen Mary. 'I am sure I am fitter to direct a campaign,' he said, 'than to manage your Houses of Lords and Commons.'

He landed at Carrickfergus towards the end of June. At once his troops realized that a new wind was blowing through the camp. 'I haven't come to Ireland to let the grass grow under my feet,' he growled.

Within less than three weeks he brought James and his smaller forces to bay. The armies faced each other across the River Boyne, a few miles from where it flowed into the Irish Sea near Drogheda.

Nothing much happened at first. An occasional musket-shot was exchanged between patrols and outposts, but things grew livelier when James's men identified William coolly sitting on the river-bank to eat some breakfast during a pause in his inspection of the lines. Orders were quickly issued and a couple of light field cannon wheeled into position. As the Dutchman stood up to remount his charger, the gunners opened fire. One ball killed a member of William's staff. A second shot ricocheted and struck William a numbing blow on the right shoulder. But he went on throughout that long summer's day, making his dispositions for the morrow's battle.

The next day dawned fine. William, a tough soldier, still under forty, took command of his own left wing, made up entirely of cavalry, and sent them into the attack. James, a much older man, with more naval experience than military, watched the battle from a hill behind his army.

For a time his French troops bore the brunt of William's assault. Old Schomberg rallied his Huguenots against them. 'Come on, messieurs, there are your persecutors!' They charged through the river at the Catholic French. Schomberg fell. William launched another wave, throwing his own Dutchmen and the Irishmen of Inniskillen into the mêlée, leading the way, sword in hand.

Superior numbers and equipment told. James's men broke, and, seeing the day was lost, the Stuart king turned his horse and rode for the safety of Dublin. Thence he fled to France, and resistance to William ceased with the surrender of Limerick a year later.

After that – despite promises of fair treatment – began those long years of persecution which understandably linger in Irish memory so hatefully. No Catholic was allowed to vote or sit in Parliament. He might not become a judge or a barrister, run a school, enter a university, hold public office, possess a gun, or own a horse worth more than £5. If he loved his freedom and dignity, and could escape abroad, he did so. More than ten thousand of the bravest and best went into exile – it was known as 'the flight of the Wild Geese' – and the rest of the population who remained were treated, as the English Earl of Chesterfield declared, worse than the Negroes in the American plantations.

This injustice continued not for a few years but for generations and goes far to explain the Irish feeling against Britain. And that is why the modern marches and celebrations by the descendants of those who won the Battle of the Boyne on 12 July 1690, are so bitterly resented by the descendants of those who, long ago, were on the losing side.

Royal Progress

'Her Majesty is determined to tarry two days at your house, that is to say tomorrow night and Thursday all day . . . You had need to consider how your provision of drink, etc., may hold out.'

It must have been with decidedly mixed feelings that Sir Francis Willoughby, of Middleton Hall in Warwickshire, read this letter one July day in the year 1575. It was signed by Sir Francis Knollys, treasurer to the royal household.

To entertain Queen Elizabeth I was at once a great honour, an alarming responsibility, and a tremendous expense. She herself ate and drank sparingly, but the warning in the letter was a reminder that she would not come alone.

When Her Majesty went on tour through her realm – a 'royal progress' was the term – she was attended by a host of officers, courtiers, servants and bodyguards, not to mention all the nobility and gentry of the area who showed their devotion by tagging on to the party.

The baggage train was like that of an army. The Queen loved clothes and had an immense wardrobe. She was apt to make snap decisions and change her mind suddenly – not only as to what she would wear but even as to where she would stay.

Woe betide her ladies if the gown or the jewels she fancied had not been packed.

Besides her dresses there were bedclothes, cushions and hangings, and countless other items. Altogether, her entourage needed about three hundred strong two-wheel carts to transport all their belongings, and because of the bad roads each cart took five or six horses to haul it.

When the Queen travelled by carriage, she grumbled that the bumpiness of those roads made her black and blue. It was more comfortable often to use a litter, slung between horses, or best of all to ride horseback like the gentlemen escorting her.

In any case, Willoughby knew he must find fodder for something like 2,000 beasts – by 'tomorrow night' – as well as food and drink for his horde of human guests.

In theory the royal household would pay for everything. He

was required merely to offer shelter. In practice he knew that it was unusual to send in a claim. The honour of entertaining Her Majesty – it was tactful to say – was sufficient recompense. Some men bankrupted themselves to outdo their rivals. There was a strong temptation to spend lavishly, for to please the Queen was the way to win titles, political power, and financial advantages.

It was in that same month of July 1575 that her favourite, the Earl of Leicester, entertained her for eighteen days with those lavish thousand-pound-a-day festivities that went down in history as 'the Princely Pleasures of Kenilworth'.

It was the hottest July anyone could remember, and ideal for the water pageant, staged on the broad lake beneath the castle walls, which was an outstanding feature of the programme. A swimming mermaid, twenty-four feet long, was ingeniously contrived. So was an immense dolphin, on which an actor rode as Arion, to deliver the usual speech of exaggerated compliments to the Queen.

Many believe that this performance was seen by Shakespeare, then an eleven-year-old schoolboy at Stratford a few miles away, and that the memory prompted his phrase in *Twelfth Night*, 'where, like Arion on the dolphin's back . . .' If so, he must have gleefully remembered also, though he did not mention it, that the actor playing Arion had steadied his nerves with too much drink beforehand and at the critical moment in the pageant, instead of reciting the prepared verses, he could not recall a word, plucked off his mask, and announced to his hilarious audience, 'I am none of Arion, not I, but honest Harry Goldingham!' No one was more amused than Elizabeth, who had a keen sense of humour.

She was tireless in making these annual journeys, which she found ideal for 'meeting the people' in a stormy age when it was vital for a sovereign to hold the loyalty and love of the population at large. Her courtiers, not unnaturally, were not so enthusiastic. A progress meant extra work and problems of many kinds. They tried to dissuade her with various excuses, such as the danger of assassination and the fatigues of travel.

The Queen would not listen. 'Let the old stay behind,' she cried scornfully, 'and the young and able go with me.' She was sixty-six herself when she said that. She died three years later, and she had kept up her custom till the end.

The Young Emperor

On 25 July 306, the soldiers of the legion were cheering wildly. They had just proclaimed the eighteen-year-old son of their dead commander as Emperor of Rome.

This scene was taking place not in the Empire's ancient capital under a hot Italian sun but far away, and much farther north, in what is now the English city of York but was then a main garrison town in the province of Britain, and was called Eboracum.

This curious fact calls for a little explanation.

The Roman Empire in those days was a vast territory, sprawling across the map from the borders of Scotland to the Sahara Desert, the Red Sea, and what is now Turkey and Arabia. This territory, which today covers so many different countries with their own governments and languages, was held together by a network of wonderful straight roads, a highly organized army, and an official language, Latin, that was everywhere understood.

Yet how difficult it was to govern such an area as a single empire will be realized if we remember that the Romans had none of our modern advantages. No news or instruction could travel faster than a galloping messenger with fresh horses provided at each post-house. The Romans had no radio, telephone, teleprinter, aircraft or printing press. Every written order had to be copied out by hand. They had not even the typewriter and the convenience of carbon paper.

Twenty years earlier, the Emperor Diocletian had come to the conclusion that no one man, however able, could control such widespread dominions from a single headquarters. He had subdivided the power. There was to be an Emperor in the West and an Emperor in the East, each with the title of 'Augustus'. And each should have a junior partner, with the title of 'Caesar', ready to step into his place when he died.

That was important. Emperors were not always succeeded by their sons. Usually they chose some man they favoured. This led to plots, quarrels, murders and civil wars. In such disputes, the man who came out on top as the new emperor was the one most popular with the soldiers – but the troops in one part of the Empire often disagreed with those of another army a thousand miles away.

This was the dangerous situation in July 306.

Just over a year earlier, the two Augusti had resigned and been succeeded by their junior partners. The new 'Emperor in the West' was Constantius, who was both a good general and an efficient, kindly ruler. As his own junior, or 'Caesar', he wanted his seventeen-year-old son, Constantine, who – young as he was – had already shown promise in his first military service. Unfortunately, Constantine was at the far side of the Empire, at the mercy of the new Emperor in the East, a man named Galerius, who wanted to block his appointment and choose both the new Caesars from among his own followers. Galerius kept Constantine almost as a hostage at his court at Nicomedia, in Asia Minor. Constantius began to suspect that Galerius was plotting to get all power, west as well as east, into his own hands.

It had not yet come to an open split. He sent a polite request to Galerius, explaining that he was preparing an expedition to Scotland, to teach the rebellious Picts a lesson, and would like to have his son's assistance. Before Galerius could think of an excuse to say no, Constantine left the palace and started a break-neck ride across Europe to join his father. He knew there was not a moment to lose. If the messengers of Galerius could overtake him there were hostile governors in the provinces who would arrest or even put him to death. Never could he have been more thankful for those straight arterial roads and the post-houses at regular intervals with the fresh mounts available to anyone riding with imperial authority. He took care to leave no horses at all for anyone who might be pursuing him.

Constantine found his father waiting for him at Boulogne. They crossed the Channel and led their troops north to repel the invading Picts. But they had no sooner won the victory and retired to the legionary base at York than Constantius fell ill and died.

His experienced officers and supporters felt they must act with decision. They were not going to let Galerius chose their new Emperor in the West. The word went round, and the troops were soon cheering young Constantine as Augustus in place of his dead father.

That youth, however, behaved with the wisdom that in after years won him the name of 'Constantine the Great'. He was not ready for an out-and-out struggle for power – yet. He wrote smoothly to Galerius. He did not himself want to be 'Augustus', only to be rightfully recognized as 'Caesar'. That much Galerius did not now dare to refuse.

Constantine was repaid for his caution. Within a few years he was unchallenged master of the Roman Empire, the founder of Constantinople, the ruler who first made Christianity the official religion of his subjects. It is a story too long to tell here, but it began on that summer day on the parade ground at York.

August

Murder in the Forest

For hundreds of years it was regarded as an accident. Today the inquiries of persistent scholars suggest that it must almost certainly have been an ingenious murder.

'Every schoolboy knows' (as Macaulay used to say) that King William II died by an arrow, while deer-hunting in the New Forest. The commonest version is that he was shot by one of his party, a French lord, Walter Tirel. What is known for certain?

On Thursday, 2 August 1100, the King and his court were staying at Castle Malwood, a big hunting lodge twenty miles from Winchester. The King had been unwell during the night. For that reason, he got up late and did not decide to go out until about six o'clock in the evening. As only about two hours of full daylight remained there was no question of going far, and the Chief Hunter, who was responsible for all the arrangements, chose a promising place within a mile of the lodge.

Deer-hunting in Norman times was nothing like stag-hunting today. The sportsmen dismounted and left their horses to their grooms. Then they went forward, bow in hand, and took up their places at intervals facing an open glade. The Chief Hunter commanded a line of beaters who advanced through the woodland, downwind, driving the deer towards the waiting marksmen.

The King duly took his stand. The party were well spread out and, using the cover of the trees, would not be able to see much, if anything, of each other. The chronicler William of Malmesbury says that 'the party split up in the woods and the King was left alone with Tirel'. But from the modern investigations of Duncan Grinnell-Milne, who paced out every yard of the ground and consulted experts on archery, deer-hunting, the New Forest, and every other subject relevant to the mystery, before publishing *The Killing of William Rufus* in 1968, it appears that even Tirel could not have seen the King from where he was standing, let alone shot him either on purpose or by accident.

Whatever happened was very swift. Within half an hour of leaving the lodge, the King lay dead with an arrow in his heart, and, as the courtiers and hunt servants ran to cluster round his body, Tirel was protesting – as he continued to insist all his life afterwards – that the arrow was not his.

Two deer, it seems, had been driven from the wood by the advancing beaters. Tirel had shot at one and missed, the King had lightly wounded the other. But, with the distance between the men, and the additional fact known to all real bowmen, that an arrow could not (as alleged) graze one target, glance off at an angle, and still have enough force to kill a man, it seems virtually certain that there was a third arrow, shot by another person. And, because of the system of hunting, it could not possibly have been an accidental shot intended for the deer.

Who was that man? His identity can hardly be established

after over eight hundred years. But there would certainly have been, standing close behind the King, hunt servants – skilful archers – whose normal duty it was to deal with wounded beasts who would otherwise escape into another part of the forest.

Under whose orders would such a man dare to shoot at the King? Only someone, it is clear, who had a powerful motive for wishing William dead and who would be in a position to hush up the affair afterwards and promise that the actual assassin would not be punished.

Only one person fits both requirements: William's younger brother, Henry.

The Conqueror had left three sons. He had bequeathed Normandy to the eldest, Robert, judging him less fit to govern England. To the youngest, Henry, he had left money but no land at all to rule.

William II, whom later generations named 'Rufus' because of his ruddy complexion, was unmarried, and so for a long time was Robert. After various quarrels – there was no love lost between any of the Conqueror's sons – they had made a treaty by which, whoever died first, the other should inherit his territory. So Henry was still cut out.

Then Robert went off on a crusade and there seemed a reasonable chance that he would never return alive. But in that summer of 1100 it was learned that he was not only safe and on his way home to Normandy but had stopped to take a bride while in Italy. Not only would he soon be back within easy reach of England, able to take over that kingdom if anything happened to William, but in due course he would probably have children. Henry's chances of ever wearing the English crown were dwindling fast. In another month or two they would be almost nil.

Henry certainly had the motive. And his swift action following the King's death were hardly those of a brother taken completely by surprise.

He was in the hunting party himself and instantly took control. Though the sun was setting, and there would be no moon, he rode hard for Winchester twenty miles away, to make sure of

120

the royal treasury located there. The late King's body was left to follow, unceremoniously, on a forest cart. It arrived at the cathedral door early the next morning. The clergy were waiting, a tomb had been opened under the central tower, a coffin was ready, and without the waste of a minute William II was lowered into his grave. Before nine o'clock, the new King Henry I was in the saddle and riding for London, seventy miles away. He arrived there at nightfall. On the following morning, little more than thirty-six hours after the loosing of the fatal arrow, he had summoned the Bishop of London to Westminster and induced him to perform the coronation ceremony. Henry argued that, whatever the arrangement made by his two brothers, he had the best right to the crown because he had been 'born in the purple', that is to say, his father had been already King of England at his birth, whereas when Robert was born the Conqueror had been only Duke of Normandy.

Henry had no trouble with the Bishop of London or with other churchmen, for they had had many disputes with the late King and Henry was now promising more favourable treatment. It is largely to these churchmen, too, that William II owes his bad reputation as one of the worst monarchs ever to rule, a man whose wickedness was punished by God through the accidental flight of an arrow. William seems to have been an effective enough ruler, no harsher than others, and popular. He was certainly his father's choice for the job, and William the Conqueror had been no fool. William II's ill-repute after his death is easiest explained as propaganda encouraged by his successor.

Exactly what happened that August evening in the forest glade can never be known with certainty, but the finger of suspicion points strongly at Henry. It is open to anyone to work out a better theory, but no one has done so yet.

A Family Row at Windsor Castle

The royal family were gathering at Windsor. Tomorrow, 21 August 1836, was the birthday of King William IV, and there was to be a banquet for a hundred guests.

Among that number was a very important young lady of seventeen, the Princess Victoria, daughter of the King's dead brother, the late Duke of Kent.

The King was looking forward to his niece's next birthday even more than to his own. His health was failing and, if he died, he had neither son nor daughter to succeed him. Victoria was next in line and would be proclaimed Queen of England. But if this should happen before May, next year, when she came of age at eighteen, there would be a short period during which her mother, the Duchess of Kent, held power in her place as regent.

That would be disastrous. King William disliked his sister-in-law, 'that nuisance of a woman', as much as he liked his little niece. He had good reason. The Duchess was tiresome and interfering, kept Victoria too much under her thumb, and deliberately obstructed the King's well-meant efforts to make friends with the girl who would inherit his throne. Nor was the King the most patient or tactful of men. Some called him 'Silly Billy'. More respectfully he was known as 'the Sailor King', for he had seen active service in the navy and still retained some of the brusque manner and colourful language of the quarterdeck.

That day, while his countless relatives were converging on Windsor, he had been to London to prorogue Parliament. He had taken the opportunity to pay a surprise call at Kensington Palace, one of the royal residences he did not himself use. His temper flared up when he found that the Duchess of Kent had calmly taken over a suite of seventeen rooms in flat defiance of his instructions.

He drove back to Windsor, fuming. The 'royals' were gathered in the state drawing-room to welcome him. He marched over to Victoria, took both her hands, and said that he wished he saw her more often. Then, turning to her mother, he bowed coldly and said in a voice that carried through the room, 'I have just come from Kensington where a most unwarrantable liberty has been taken with one of my palaces. I cannot understand conduct so disrespectful to me, and I won't endure it.'

There was an appalled silence. The Duchess made no answer. The King said no more. But the following evening at the banquet, when he rose to thank them for drinking his health, he returned to the subject.

He hoped and prayed, he declared, that at least he would be spared until the Princess Victoria came of age next year, 'so that there will be no risk of a regency by a person now near me' – the detested Duchess was in fact sitting at his right hand – 'who is surrounded by evil advisers and who is herself incompetent to act with propriety in the station in which she would be placed'.

Any other family gathering would have broken up in disorder. But no one could interrupt the King. He raged on, and the brilliant company could only sit in paralysed silence along the tables.

'I have no hesitation in saying that I have been grossly and continuously insulted by that person – but I am determined no longer to endure a course of behaviour so disrespectful to me.' He complained particularly that 'this young lady' (he glanced down at the tearful Victoria who sat facing him) had been deliberately kept away from his court, though she ought always to have been present. 'I am fully resolved this shall not happen again. I would have her know that I am King and I am determined to make my authority respected. For the future I shall insist and command that the Princess do upon all occasions appear at my court, as it is her duty to do.'

It was a birthday party that nobody ever forgot.

William was not disobeyed again. His hope and prayer were granted – just. He lived to see Victoria's eighteenth birthday on 24 May 1837. A month later, on 20 June, as though he had clung to life merely to spite his sister-in-law, he died.

Revolt in Norfolk

Today Mousehold Heath is still what it has been for centuries, a great open space northeast of Norwich, offering the splendid view of that city which was once a favourite subject for the painters of peaceful landscapes.

That scene, however, was far from peaceful in 1549, when for weeks the Heath was an encampment for a rebel army and finally a battlefield, on 27 August, on which thousands died.

The story began early in July at the little market-town of Wymondham, ten miles away. The annual festival brought crowds. After a few drinks a noisy discussion began about the hardness of the times.

Hard the times certainly were. Great changes were taking place in England, nowhere more than in Norfolk, and those changes brought suffering to many.

Prices were soaring. They were double what old people could remember at the beginning of the century. The gentry were taking over the open common lands and putting fences round them, so that the smaller folk had nowhere to graze their stock. The big farmers were going in for sheep, which required much less labour than corn-growing. There was unemployment – but in the reign of Edward VI there was no welfare state, and the unwanted worker must either beg or starve.

That noisy discussion at Wymondham ended in uproar. The crowd streamed out into the countryside and began tearing down the new fences that had robbed them of their livelihood.

They found a natural leader in Robert Kett. He was not himself a poor man, but a tanner and an owner of land. He had education and intelligence. He knew that nothing would be achieved by blind rage and disorder. He believed that if the true facts were realized by the boy King – or rather his guardians, since Edward was not yet twelve years old – then justice would be done. He had no ambition to overthrow the King or his government.

Helped by his brother, William, he managed to bring the riotous bands under control. They set up a camp on Mousehold Heath. More and more armed parties came streaming in from all over Norfolk, until 20,000 were gathered. They made themselves huts with turf walls and roofs of branches. Good discipline was kept. Every day Kett held a court of justice, sitting under a tree called the Oak of Reformation. He made the Mayor of Norwich sit beside him to see that everything was done properly. Land-owners were brought in for trial and, if found guilty of stealing common land from the people, they were held prisoners. Kett's firmness saved them from being lynched by the wilder rebels.

A petition was prepared and sent to London. It asked that lords of the manor should be prevented from enclosing common land for themselves. Field rents should be 'frozen' at the amounts charged when Henry VII became King. Other demands included free education for poor children and the dismissal of parsons who did not fulfil their duties. The Norfolk rebels were, on the whole, very serious God-fearing men.

The King's herald brought an answer to Kett beneath the Oak of Reformation. He promised nothing but a pardon if they would all go home quietly.

'Kings are wont to pardon wicked persons,' retorted Kett, 'not innocent and just men. We have done nothing to deserve such pardon. We have been guilty of no crime.'

The situation began to look uglier. The King's uncle and

guardian, Protector Somerset, had missed the chance of a reasonable settlement and came under pressure from other lords wanting to take a tough line. Kett, in turn, found it harder to hold back the more violent of his followers.

The day after the herald's departure the rebels broke into Norwich and there was some fighting. They seized control of the city but later moved out to their camp again.

There was no regular army in those days, but the Government happened to be mustering troops – many of them hired foreigners – to fight against Scotland. A small force of Italians was therefore sent under the command of the Earl of Northampton. He rode into Norwich and ordered the gates to be closed against Kett's men. This made them so angry that they attacked the city, captured an Italian officer and hanged him on the Heath. The next day they stormed the walls and, after fierce fighting and heavy casualties, sent the Earl running for his life.

Now the fat was really in the fire. The Government shelved its plan to attack Scotland and sent its forces, mainly Germans under the Earl of Warwick, to collect the remnants of Northampton's column and move on Norwich. The advance guard fought their way to the market-place, taking sixty prisoners, who were promptly hanged. But as Kett and his men withdrew to Mousehold Heath they managed to capture Warwick's guns and ammunition carts. This loss, however, was made good when the main body of the Earl's army caught up with him.

The battle that followed a day or two later was sheer massacre. The Earl was still outnumbered – his main strength lay in a mere 1,500 Germans and Italians, but these were trained, well-equipped, professional cut-throats. He had cavalry and some guns, whereas the rebels had no skill to use those they had captured. They were mown down by artillery-fire and then, when they broke and ran, ridden down by the pursuing horsemen. For three miles the ground was strewn with bodies. More than three thousand died that day.

The Ketts did not fall in the battle but were captured shortly afterwards. Robert was hanged from the walls of Norwich,

William in their own town of Wymondham, and other leaders dangled from that very Oak of Reformation in whose shade they had tried to argue their case with the King's herald. The enclosures of the common land continued, and the country population of England suffered an injustice from which they never recovered.

Wedding at Holyrood

On 8 August 1503, the townsfolk of Edinburgh crowded round Holyrood Abbey and the royal palace newly built beside it, and watched the nobility of Scotland assembling in all their splendour for a wedding fated to have even greater consequences for their country than anyone planned.

Their king, James IV, was marrying Margaret Tudor, daughter of Henry VII of England.

Their marriage had been under discussion for years, ever since Margaret was six, for it seemed a good way to ensure peace between the two kingdoms. Now Margaret was thirteen and just old enough, by the standards of those days, for the match to take place.

King James was thirty – charming, intelligent, energetic, open-handed and open-hearted, a great fighter and a great lover, the most capable of all the Stuart monarchs and the most popular with his subjects. He played the lute and travelled nowhere without his own musicians. He brought the culture of the Renaissance to the court of Scotland. He had already given Scotland a third university, at Aberdeen, at a time when England had only two. And in a few more years he was to establish in Edinburgh his country's first printing press, making books more plentifully available.

When he rode forth to welcome his young bride to Scotland he was splendidly arrayed in a crimson velvet jacket bordered with cloth-of-gold. He had sent specially to France for a whole wardrobe of expensive robes, and his lords, taking their cue from him, vied with each other in magnificence. It was an eye-opener for the Englishmen escorting their princess. They were apt to patronize Scotland as a poor, northern, barbaric land, but James and his courtiers surprised them.

It was a skilful move, too, to put on this show to impress Margaret. She was obsessed with clothes herself. It was she who introduced to Scotland the fashion of the 'gable' headdress worn by the queens shown still on our playing cards.

For the wedding itself – as on other public occasions when a king and queen appeared together – it was usual for them to dress in clothes of the same material. So James presented her with her wedding gown of white damask flowered with gold, lined and bordered with crimson velvet, and had an outfit of his own to match. The bride wore her long fair hair floating loosely over her shoulders, with a rich netted tissue veil falling to her feet, held in place by a golden crown studded with pearls and precious stones, also given her by the King.

Before that time, the Queen of Scotland had never sat beside the King on his throne. Sometimes she had stood – at most, she had been allowed a little stool. It was typical of James that he broke this tradition and ordered a chair like his own to be provided for his wife.

It would be pleasant to record that the marriage, so happily begun, continued in the same way. It would not be true. It was no romantic love-match and in the first years Margaret was too much the immature child to satisfy a full-blooded, full-living man like James. She bore no child for several years and then had three still-born babies in succession, until at last she gave him the living heir who was to become James V. Nor did the marriage succeed in its political object, to create a lasting friendship between Scotland and England, for just ten years later, in August 1513, James gathered the finest army any Scottish king had ever commanded, and led them across the Tweed. He enjoyed just two weeks of victorious advance, capturing the English castles that defied him. Then came the disastrous battle of Flodden, which developed into a massacre, costing thousands of Scottish lives including the King's and the flower of the nobility. That black day is still fittingly commemorated in the famous lament, *The flowers of the forest are a' wede away*.

Margaret did not lament long. Well within a year of her widowhood, on 6 August 1514 – just two days before the anniversary of that first wedding at Holyrood – she took the Earl of Angus as her second husband. Thirteen years later she divorced him and married a third time.

Had that first marriage come to nothing, then? Far from it. Through their son, James V, she and the King were to have a very famous granddaughter, Mary Queen of Scots. And it was Mary's son, James VI, who became James I of England in 1603 because Elizabeth I had died childless. So, unexpectedly, that August wedding in Edinburgh which had failed to keep peace between the countries had the effect, exactly one hundred years afterwards, of uniting them under the same king.

Battle on the Beach

The weather in August 55 B.C. seems to have been about as unreliable as millions of British holidaymakers have found it in modern times.

Julius Caesar had spent the previous three years in what is now France, beating down the resistance of the Gallic tribes with an iron hand and bringing their country under the sway of the Roman Republic. That summer he felt he could spare time to administer a sharp slap, if no more, to any barbarian neighbours who disturbed the order he was so harshly establishing in his territory.

First he made a raid into Germany. He astounded the wild warriors across the Rhine by building – in ten days – a timber bridge across the broad, swift-flowing river behind which they had felt themselves quite safe. His legionaries poured over (the bridge was forty feet wide), spent just eighteen days ravaging the countryside, and dismantled the whole construction when they withdrew.

Caesar's raid on Britain, that same summer, was designed as a similar operation, only with ships instead of a bridge.

The Britons were Celts, closely related to the Gauls, whom they had helped against the Romans. Caesar wanted to punish them for this and discourage them from helping in any Gallic liberation movement. He was also curious to see this island on the edge of the known world, and knew that a victory there would help his political career in Rome, where a few years later he was to make himself dictator. But he had no idea of staying on the island and conquering it. The Roman conquest of Britain came ninety-eight years later, in A.D. 43.

What with his expedition into Germany, and then the uncertain weather in the Channel, it was not until late August that Caesar was able to start.

He had gathered a fleet of troopships and transports at Bononia (now Boulogne) and there he embarked two legions, some cavalry, and the heavy equipment such as giant catapults and engineering implements he might need.

He could see the island across the water, a pale line of green downs and cheese-pale cliffs. He knew a certain amount about it, for, with spies, travelling merchants and contacts with various discontented Britons who were prepared to collaborate with an invader, it was not hard to build up a picture. He knew that the country was divided between many petty kings and tribes, often at odds with each other. The Britons were formidable fighters but they had not the strict discipline of the Romans.

The Britons, in turn, knew that the Romans were coming,

though they could not foresee exactly where they would land. That August the tribes of southeastern Britain made ready for resistance.

They must not be imagined as naked savages, painted blue with woad, as the old history-books used to describe them. Caesar wrote of them going into battle 'naked' but he meant only that they did not wear body armour like his legionaries and that they laid aside their heavy tartan plaids which might have hindered them.

The Britons had splendid bronze helmets and embossed shields, brilliantly coloured with enamels. They wore trousers of linen, long-sleeved tunics, cloaks or plaids or animal skins, and leather shoes. Their gold bracelets, brooches and torques (or neck ornaments), prove that they had fine artists and craftsmen.

It is a pity that we do not know the exact day on which Caesar sailed against them. It is the first event in British history that can be even roughly dated. It was near the end of the month.

The most probable place where Caesar landed is Walmer, near Deal, on the Kentish coast.

At one moment it looked as though he might not be able to land at all. He had relied on his artillery to give covering fire by hurling stones and javelins, but the transport vessels on which his catapults were mounted became detached from the invasion fleet during the short crossing and were not there to support his infantry.

Tightly packed in their ships, the legionaries found themselves faced with a terrifying horde of tall, fiercely moustached Britons, who seemed to cover the beach and came wading out into the shallow water brandishing their swords and spears.

Used as they were to fighting on land in close formation, precisely according to the drill-book, the Romans hesitated. Then it was (as Caesar's own book on the campaign relates) that the standard-bearer of the Tenth Legion mounted the ship's rail, called on his comrades to follow him, and jumped down into the waves. To lose the eagle-topped standard would have meant undying shame to the regiment. So, without further hesitation, the legionaries went spilling over the side, and in no time the troops in the other vessels were doing the same.

There was a ferocious struggle before enough of the Romans could wade ashore and form up in their usual compact mass, throwing their short spears and stabbing with their swords. At last, however, they won a beachhead. More and more men disembarked. Unable to drive them back into the sea, the Britons withdrew inland.

Caesar's first 'invasion' was a brief affair. He had not a big enough army to venture far, and the season was near its end. The Britons lurked in the forests and fought him with guerrilla tactics. Roman patrols and foraging parties suffered ambushes and hit-and-run raids. The Britons had a mobile weapon new to the Romans – the light, swift-moving, two-wheeled war chariot, which could bring up a fighting man, let him throw his spears, and whisk him out of danger before the Romans could reply. Caesar had not even the cavalry to deal with this threat.

Used to the Mediterranean, the Romans did not like the rough northern seas with their high tides. And the autumn gales were near at hand. So Caesar went back to Gaul before the crossing became any more dangerous. At once he started preparations for a more ambitious expedition the following summer.

He had shown that it could be done. That battle on the Kentish beach in August 55 B.C. foreshadowed an era of Roman rule in Britain which would last for centuries.

September

London's Burning

For the rest of their lives the Londoners never forgot the great fire that started in the early hours of Sunday morning, 2 September 1666.

It began in a bakery in Pudding Lane, near London Bridge. At first nobody realized its seriousness. Pepys (who gives a splendid eyewitness account in his diary) tells how his maid-servant Jane woke him at three o'clock, and how he slipped into his 'nightgown', or dressing-gown, and went to look at the distant glare from her bedroom window – and then returned to his own bed and slept without any idea of the disaster to come.

There were no fire brigades in Charles II's reign. The house-holder and his anxious neighbours were left to deal with the situation themselves. Fire buckets of wood or leather were usually kept ready at the parish church, along with long-handled iron hooks for pulling down thatch. Not until ten years later was the 'fire engine' introduced from Holland – and even then it was a feeble, hand-operated device, handicapped by the lack of water mains.

The buildings of those days also encouraged the swift spread of the flames. There was much timber in their construction, much tarring and pitching for their preservation. Space was precious. Houses were crammed tightly together, and the overhanging upper storeys jutted out and almost met each other across the narrow lanes.

To cap everything, this particular fire started near the riverside in an area full of merchants' warehouses containing vast stocks of oil, tallow, spirits and equally inflammable goods.

When day broke through the smoke pall and drifting smuts, it was clear to all that this was no ordinary fire. Three hundred houses had been destroyed, the blaze was still spreading, and the flames were crackling their way along the buildings that lined the arches of London Bridge.

By this time the Lord Mayor was bestirring himself and trying to organize counter-measures. It was a difficult task. People were – naturally enough – most concerned to save their own shops and houses, or, if they could not, at least get their furniture and goods away to safety. There was no fire insurance, just as there was no social security. A man who lost his house and possessions could be reduced to beggary if he had no generous friends or relatives and owned nothing outside London.

With that fearful thought in mind, no one was keen to leave his own premises and fight the fire in another part of the town.

For the same reason, when the King sent orders to the Lord Mayor to pull down houses and create gaps, like fire-breaks in a forest, to check the spread of the flames, a man whose own house was not yet alight was reluctant to see it deliberately demolished.

The Lord Mayor was collapsing with exhaustion. The King's brother, the Duke of York, later James II, set a good example by riding up and down with his bodyguard, to prevent looting and panic. Dockyard workers were brought in from Woolwich and Deptford to help the troops in the demolition work. Gunpowder was used to hasten matters. On Tuesday night – the fire still raging after three days – there was a succession of explosions along Tower Street as the authorities strove to protect the great fortress by levelling the houses near by.

All this time, the roads leading from the city were choked with laden carts and refugees bowed under their burdens. The river was crowded with lighters, removing goods by water. Many people who had patches of garden dug holes and buried their wine and other possessions that they could not take to safety.

The air snowed white ash and wisps of charred material – scraps of silk were picked up in the Chiltern Hills, carried thirty miles by the wind that so fatally fanned the conflagration. The streets of London were carpeted with rubble so hot that it scorched men's shoes. There were sights of terrifying grandeur, as when the leaden roof of St Paul's melted and gushed like lava into the church below. There was pathos – Pepys noted how the pigeons, as reluctant as the citizens to quit their homes, flew hither and thither distractedly until their wings were burnt and they fell into the fire.

For four days the terror lasted. Then it ceased and men could begin to count the cost.

There had been many great fires before in the country's history. In 1136 medieval London had been devastated from St Paul's to the Bridge. Countless other towns, large and small, had suffered similarly – at Shakespeare's Stratford in 1614 fifty-four houses had been destroyed in the space of two hours – but the Great Fire of London was unique in scale.

The city was a blackened ruin from near the Tower to the western end of Fleet Street. Four hundred streets and alleys had gone, 13,200 houses, St Paul's and eighty-nine parish churches, the Guildhall and scores of other public buildings. Of London's half million population about 200,000 were homeless.

Christopher Wren set to work at once, 'took an exact survey of the whole area' and 'designed a plan or model of a new city, in which the deformity and inconveniences of the old town were remedied . . .'

Wren's grand design was never carried out, but his domed St Paul's and some at least of his fifty-two rebuilt parish churches remain as evidence of the elegant new London he helped to create on the ashes of the old.

The Sporting Colonel

One Sunday morning in 1814, it was 4 September to be exact, the elegant Regency ladies and gentlemen of Southampton, as they paraded after church, were treated to a sight even more entertaining than each other.

Colonel Thomas Thornton and party were embarking for France.

This was not in itself remarkable. In that summer of 1814 the Continent had been re-opened to British tourists for the first time after ten years of war. Now Napoleon had abdicated and was an exile on the island of Elba. In the past few months countless British people had crossed the Channel to tour the Europe so long denied to them, and many had gone by way of Southampton.

Colonel Thornton, however, was no ordinary tourist. That had been clear from the moment of his arrival in the town on the Friday evening.

In that period, when it was usual to display one's wealth and rank as conspicuously as possible, it was not uncommon for an English milord – or even a gentleman of means like the Colonel – to travel in a miniature convoy of carriages and with several servants. Southampton had seen other important persons setting forth with three carriages, a coachman, two grooms, a house-keeper, a chief butler, and other staff. To take ten horses was not unknown, though most people hired from the post-houses along the foreign roads. But Southampton was not used to seeing a tourist accompanied by one hundred and twenty hounds and dogs (including the pick of the royal buck hounds) along with three hawks, a falconer, a keeper and dog-feeders.

Who, they asked, as we might ask too, was this sporting colonel?

Thornton, who earned himself a long piece in the *Dictionary of National Biography*, was an extreme example of those eccentrics, always a law to themselves, who were free to flourish in the eighteenth and nineteenth centuries.

Born in 1757, he had been a colonel in the Yorkshire militia and was not a professional soldier. Far from serving against Napoleon, he greatly admired him, had once presented him with a brace of pistols, and had tried to become a French citizen. France and sport were his two enthusiasms, combined in a book he had written called *A Sporting Tour in France*. Now he was planning to settle in that country.

Thornton had a passionate temper and gave a fine display of it that weekend. Just before leaving his Wiltshire home, he had engaged in a furious row with his huntsman, a character of equal independence, and the two men had thrashed each other with their whips. Now, arrived in Southampton, the huntsman led a strike of the servants, who refused to embark for France until the Colonel granted their demands. The Colonel however pro-duced a lawyer and so frightened them that they all gave in except the huntsman, who was promptly sacked and left to go home on foot.

In high good humour the Colonel then resolved to fly his hawks in the open fields outside the town. He was the man who had revived, in the late eighteenth century, the forgotten sport of falconry – he had given the name, *Falcon*, to a sloop in which he had cruised round the Scottish coast, landing to hunt, shoot, fish and fly his birds.

So, that Saturday, a crowd of two thousand townspeople were given a demonstration of falconry – and the Colonel's fury.

A fine heron was sighted three miles away. The falconer released his bird – and it promptly vanished. Neither heron nor hawk was seen again, though the falconer went on calling for half an hour. The incident is preserved in a journal kept by Matthew Todd, valet to the Colonel's nephew, who was in the party. 'The Colonel' (Todd records) 'fell into a great passion and swore he would skin the falconer alive if he did not recover the hawk.' Fortunately, by getting up at four o'clock the next morning, the man was able to find the bird, and the Colonel, his temper restored, rewarded him with a gold sovereign.

The party was far too large to cross the Channel by ordinary packet. It required a ship to itself, if not an ark. The Colonel inspected several vessels and chartered one to carry him and his complete 'Establishment' – Matthew Todd always used a respectful capital letter to denote this extraordinary party – to Rouen. True to character, the Colonel beat down the owners from £150 to £130.

The bargain settled, the Establishment began to embark while the church bells were summoning more conventional folk to morning service. Horses and hounds were coaxed up the gangway, the Colonel's thirty guns carefully stowed, the three carriages securely lashed on deck, including an odd one designed to transport a boat. Then the anchor was weighed, sail hoisted, and the ship put to sea to the cheers and waves of thousands of people crowding the Pier Head.

'When fairly on our way,' writes Todd, 'the Colonel pulls off his hat to Old England, returns thanks for all the sporting amusement it had afforded him, bids farewell to it, and wishes he may never see it again.'

It took them thirty hours to reach Havre at the mouth of the

Seine, and everyone was 'uncommonly sick excepting' (of course) 'the Colonel'. That gentleman was so fully himself that he was ready for another tremendous row with the ship's captain, who wanted him to disembark there because the river was not deep enough for the vessel to sail up to Rouen. The Colonel refused to pay his bill, the Captain complained to the shipping officers ashore, and they seized the horses and carriages as security. 'But the Colonel, more used to the business of contracts than either the Captain or the whole party put together,' won the argument and got £30 taken off the bill.

They then landed, the gentlemen donning their hunting pink, and set off in procession along the road to Rouen, astonishing the French populace no less than the Southampton people. Some thought the Colonel was the Prince Regent, others that he was the British ambassador, and his arrival in Rouen threw the whole town into commotion.

The Knockshinnoch Rescue

Mining disasters provide some of the most dramatic episodes in the history of workaday life. Nothing is more sudden, nothing creates more suspense, nothing produces more stories of comradeship and heroism. One such story is that of the Knockshinnoch rescue, which began on 7 September 1950.

The first hint of trouble was a telephone call to the manager, Mr Halliday, which brought him hurrying back to his office.

Knockshinnoch Castle was a coal-mine in the Scottish lowlands. It stood in Ayrshire, on the verge of the Robert Burns country, still a pleasant landscape despite the pit-heads and other marks of industry. The scarlet-berried rowan-trees brighten the hedgerows. The stream Burns knew, his 'sweet Afton', runs through the fields only a quarter of a mile from the colliery.

There was nothing sweet about the Afton that day. After days of heavy rain it was in spate. The rowans bent against the Atlantic gale. The smoke writhed over the glistening house-roofs of New Cumnock close by. The pastures were water-logged.

Andrew Houston, the overman in charge, quickly told the manager all he knew. There had been a fall in the No. 5 Heading. Suspecting trouble on the surface, he had found, sure enough, a hole in an adjacent field, clear evidence of subsidence. He had sent the colliery blacksmith to fence it in.

Having handed over to Mr Halliday, the overman went down to see what was happening below. But the next alarm came from the blacksmith. He had gone to fetch more timber. Returning to the hole in the field, he found that it had become a huge crater. His fence had vanished. Barely had he told his story than eight breathless and shaken miners arrived on the surface. They had just escaped with their lives. They had heard a rushing noise, then the walls had caved in, and a mass of sludge had come at

them. They had downed tools and run before it. It had slopped and tumbled after them, faster and faster, like some half-solid tidal wave.

Eight men had got away. But somewhere behind all those tons of earth and sludge, blocking the West Mine tunnel, the rest of the afternoon shift were buried alive – one hundred and twenty-eight of them, together with Houston, the overman. And every minute, as the rainstorm flogged the surface of the land above, more and more debris was being washed down to seal their grave.

Mr Halliday went down and saw the situation with his own eyes. Then his office became the operational headquarters for the rescue attempt. Telephone calls went out to doctors, police, rescue brigades and everyone who could help.

At ten o'clock that night there was an incoming call which gave them all fresh heart. A calm voice said: 'This is Houston, speaking from No. 5 Heading. We're all here, bar thirteen.' Every escape route was blocked, he went on. He had explained matters to the men, warned them that they might be trapped for a long time, and made them switch off their lamps.

On the surface men worked with redoubled energy. The crater must be plugged, so that at least no more debris slid down into the mine. Volunteers flocked to the scene. All through that black, blustery night they toiled, rolling tree-trunks and beams into the hole. Whole haystacks were thrown down in bales. At dawn the engineers rigged up a conveyor-belt, running four hundred yards from pit-head to crater, transporting tons of material. At last the creeping flow of sludge was halted.

Meanwhile the agent, Mr Bone, knew the lay-out of the disused Bank Mine near by. At one point, he said, only twenty-four feet of coal separated the workings of the two pits. But after seven years' closure, with no ventilation, gas had accumulated in the abandoned working and it was impossible to get within a quarter of a mile of the place where they must dig to break through to the trapped men. Fans had to be installed. By half-past eight in the morning the gas had dispersed enough for work to begin.

But it remained an ever-present danger, and, what particularly worried the rescuers, when a hole was bored through to their mates the gas might rush through it and suffocate them.

Andrew Houston was calmly telephoning the surface at fifteen-minute intervals. He received instructions now to take a party of volunteers and reconnoitre the section which ran so close to the neighbouring mine. Soon he was on the line again. They had reached the place without difficulty. So only eight yards of solid wall divided them from their rescuers.

Digging began on both sides. Hungry, thirsty and weary, the imprisoned men worked valiantly in relays of five. At four o'clock in the afternoon their anxious listening was rewarded by the sound of picks on the other side. But it was too far to the left, the tunnellers were going to miss each other, with tragic waste of time and effort. Houston hurried back to his telephone and rang the office above. The rescuers began again. By midnight there was a small bore-hole connecting the two parties, and mercifully no sign that the draught would carry the gas through.

On the surface the colliery siren signalled the good news to the crowds waiting in the darkness. But the ordeal was by no means finished, even when the bore-hole was enlarged enough for food, drink and blankets to be passed to the beleaguered men. Dumbfounded, they learned that they must stay where they were – even let the hole be blocked up again, so that the ventilation system could clear the gas in the other mine.

Gas was the problem still. It was continually gathering in the disused workings. To reach safety involved a two-mile walk underground, and for half a mile the atmosphere was too poisonous to enter without breathing apparatus. All Scotland was being scoured to collect enough apparatus for so large a number of men. Some might be flown from America. It was a race against time.

It says much for the discipline of the trapped miners that every one accepted the situation at once. They were strengthened by the example of a local official, David Park, who had done no similar rescue-work for ten years. He squeezed through the hole, explained the problem, and said he would stay with them until they were out. Then the hole was sealed up.

'What counted most of all,' Houston said afterwards, 'was that he was there – and stayed there.'

On Saturday afternoon, about forty-eight hours after the start of the emergency, enough Salvus breathing apparatus had been collected to equip each man. With perfect discipline, in strict order of age, they began to file out, led by the sixty-eight-year-old James Haddon. In the manager's office the telephone rang once more. 'The last man has left,' said David Park, 'and I am just about to follow.'

The disaster had been great enough. The thirteen men, missing at the start, were never found. But the main body, by fortitude and self-control, with the help of an innumerable host of allies outside, had come through their ordeal without further casualty, and one of the proudest pages had been added to the chronicle of British mining.

His Worship the Mayor

Ever since anyone could remember, they had chosen the new Mayor at Michaelmas. The proceedings had started with a solemn church service at the parish church of St Mary and ended – rather less soberly – with much drinking and merriment, with red-faced aldermen tossing back the liquor at the cost of the Town Corporation.

There was nothing remarkable in that. All the ancient towns of England did much the same.

But this time, in Nottingham, on 29 September 1682, there was an air of expectancy. The outgoing Mayor, Gervas Wylde, did not stir from his house for the procession to church, where the Town Clerk and half the councillors were already assembled. The other half – the Mayor's Tory supporters – clustered round his door, ready to escort him when he gave the word. But still he dallied.

Meanwhile, in his newly-rebuilt castle on its rock at the other end of the town, the Duke of Newcastle strained his ears for the first sounds of disorder in the distance. His men stood ready for action. As Lord Lieutenant of Nottinghamshire, the representative of King Charles II himself, the Duke was responsible for keeping the peace that day.

And the man for whom they were all waiting – a messenger with a parchment bearing the royal seal – was at that moment urging his horse along the last weary mile of causeway across the meadows between Trent Bridge and the town.

Why was everybody expecting trouble? To understand that, it is necessary to look back over the preceding year or two.

Charles II, now nearing the end of his reign, was trying to make sure (since he had no heir to succeed him) that his Roman Catholic brother should become King James II. Every time Parliament passed a law to disqualify James, Charles dissolved Parliament and ordered a general election, only to find that the new Parliament was just as determined to ban his brother.

This happened in 1679, 1680 and 1681. The King and his Tory supporters were always beaten by the Whig party.

In those days very few men had votes. In towns like Nottingham it was really the two or three dozen councillors who picked the Member of Parliament. If by hook or by crook the King could gradually get the councils packed with his own supporters he would have a Parliament equally willing to vote as he wished.

There had been some shifty work in Nottingham during the past year.

The King had sent the Corporation a letter recommending them to elect one of his supporters, William Petty, to fill a vacant seat as alderman. But the worthy citizens did not like even the King to tell them how to run their own business, so they

147

defiantly elected someone else, and Mr Petty received only a single vote.

Clearly the King would never get the kind of M.P.s he wanted by trying (and failing) to get single councillors elected in various towns. A surer and better method was to set up brand-new councils of hand-picked members certain to vote the right way.

There was one snag. The towns had ancient charters granted by other kings long ago. Somehow they must be persuaded to give up these old charters, giving them the right to manage their own affairs, and accept new charters in exchange.

All that year Gervas Wylde had been playing the King's game. In July, without warning, he had surprised the Council with a proposition to surrender the ancient town charter and accept another. Tories and Whigs had tied, fourteen votes to fourteen. The Mayor had forced the resolution through by using his casting vote.

Hundreds of townspeople had signed a protest. He had ignored it. The Town Clerk, the local gentry, the clergy, and many of the common folk were hotly opposed to his giving away their liberties. Complaints were sent to the Lord Chancellor and the Attorney-General in London, but no notice was taken.

Now it was the date to elect a new mayor. It was vital for the Tory scheme that another of their party should take the place of Wylde, and this man, William Toplady, would be named in the new charter. Unfortunately, the charter had not arrived.

Without it, the Council would choose a more popular senior alderman, William Greaves, for Toplady was much junior in standing, and voting did not follow exact party lines in those days.

Greaves's supporters left the church and came down to the Mayor's house, demanding that the ceremony begin. The Mayor was still playing for time when his Sergeant-at-Mace brought the news that the charter had at last arrived.

The Mayor's attitude changed. Word was sent to the Town Clerk, waiting in the church, to come to the Council Chamber and read the charter officially. He did not budge. He was sent for again. He remained obstinate.

148

'I know there is an old charter,' he said, 'and what I am by that charter. But I do not know of any new one.'

The Tory group decided to ignore him. They went over to the Council Chamber, read the new charter themselves, and were just about to proclaim the election of William Toplady as the new Mayor when their opponents stormed into the building.

A tremendous fight ensued. The Whigs threw the Tories out of the Council Chamber. The Tories retreated to Wylde's house and finished the election there. But when they announced the result in the streets, at the old market cross, rioting broke out again.

'No new charter!' one alderman was bawling. 'It's not worth a groat!'

One of the town sergeants received what he described in court afterwards as 'a full swop over the face' and a former Tory mayor had his waistcoat ruined as he tried to protect the precious new document.

The fighting only stopped when the Duke and his men came charging down from the Castle. Twenty-three worthy Whig townsmen were arrested, charged with rioting, and tried before the notorious Judge Jeffreys, who imposed heavy fines on all but one of them.

So, for the time being, the people of Nottingham (and some other towns) lost their rights to self-government and the King's brother was able, three years later, to inherit the crown. But 1688 brought 'the Glorious Revolution', and soon the town's ancient privileges were restored.

October

Trafalgar Day

Trafalgar Day, 21 October, is one of the few patriotic anniversaries ever remembered by the British, who are not much given to celebrating national victories of long ago.

Even so, those people who recall it – especially people with a pride and interest in the Royal Navy – probably do not so much celebrate the occasion for the sake of the battle as for the man connected with it.

Nelson, the little man with the blind eye and the missing arm, still dominates the London square named after his last triumph. There he stands on his column, 145 feet above the tourists squinting up to see his cocked-hatted silhouette against the drifting clouds. Nelson, with his indomitable courage, his warm human gestures, his romantic love-affair with Lady Hamilton, has caught and held the imagination of the world. Not only in Britain but in unlikely countries like the Soviet Union the Nelson legend is powerfully alive today.

In October 1805, Britain was locked in the conflict with Napoleon's France, which ended only at Waterloo nearly ten years later. Napoleon was master of mainland Europe and (like Hitler in a similar position in 1940) considered an invasion of Britain to knock out the last nation that defied him. He had joined the Spanish fleet to his own. It was vital that the British should not lose command of the sea to this powerful partnership of enemies.

Without radio and other twentieth-century aids, it was extremely difficult to be sure where those enemies were. Blockading their ports with sailing ships, week after week, was hard enough

– but once the hostile fleet could slip out into the open Atlantic finding it again was like searching a forest for a fugitive.

That was why Nelson, having at last tracked down his quarry to Cadiz, the great port in southern Spain, was desperately anxious to tempt it out to sea so that he could destroy it before the winter began and made his blockade more difficult.

Villeneuve, the French admiral, had the slightly bigger fleet, thirty-three French or Spanish sail-of-the-line and seven frigates, against Nelson's thirty-two and five. Villeneuve was no coward. Nelson had fought him before. Nelson was sure that, given a chance, Villeneuve would come out. He drew up his plans accordingly.

Sure enough, on 19 October, the enemy were sighted putting to sea. Quietly the British sailors began the grim preparations for the battle that was now certain.

Decks were cleared for action. The rows of cannon were checked, not least the ropes that took the force of the recoil when they were fired – for if a gun broke loose it was as dangerous as a stampeding bull. Buckets of water were made ready to drench the barrels when they grew too hot, or to douse any fire that started. Cannon-balls and other kinds of shot were placed handy, but the actual explosive – the gunpowder – had to remain for safety in its deep hold below the waterline, whence half-naked boys, the 'powder monkeys', would race to fetch it as needed when the fight began.

Grimmest of all were the surgeon's preparations. He went down to the cockpit where the midshipmen had their living quarters. Their sea-chests were placed together and covered with an old sail to form an operating table. Buckets were set round it to receive the mangled arms and legs that he expected to amputate. Bottles of rum and gin were handy to dull the pain of the sufferer, and there was a leather gag for him to bite on while the surgeon was using his knife or saw.

While all this work was going on, men seized any free moment to send off letters which might well be their last. On Nelson's flagship, the *Victory*, a coxwain was so busy preparing the mail-bags

that he forgot to include his own letter to his wife. Nelson
heard what had happened. The mail-ship had gone. 'Hoist a
signal to bring her back,' he ordered. 'Who knows but that he
may fall in action tomorrow? His letter shall go with the rest.'
The vessel came back for that single letter. It was human gestures
like that – despite all the terrifying responsibilities on his mind –
that made Nelson beloved by his men.

Everyone knows of that other signal he ordered before battle
was joined: 'England expects that every man will do his duty.'
Everyone knows that it was Nelson himself who fell in action,
picked off by a French sniper in the rigging of the *Redoubtable*
alongside as he walked the quarterdeck of the *Victory*, careless of
danger. And famous artists have made familiar his dying moments
in that grisly cockpit below decks. 'Thank God, I have done my
duty,' were the last words he uttered.

He had. His plan had brilliantly succeeded. The enemy had lost nineteen ships captured and another blown up. Villeneuve was one of 12,000 prisoners.

Less than five hundred men of Nelson's fleet died in the battle. But Nelson himself was one of them, and for most people that loss dimmed the brightness of his achievement.

It took them time to grasp the full meaning of what had happened. Napoleon's sea-power was broken and never threatened Britain again. And in fact it would be a hundred years before any other country – the Kaiser's German Empire in 1914 – could even think of doing battle with the British Navy.

No one could know that in October 1805. But the death of Nelson was something they could all understand.

The Smugglers

One night at the beginning of October 1747, when George II was king, sixty desperate-looking men gathered in a glade of Charlton Forest near Chichester in Sussex. They were armed with pistols, carbines and blunderbusses, and they were in an ugly mood. There and then they signed an agreement to break open His Majesty's Custom House at Poole, in Dorset, and remove all the goods locked up inside – notably an immense consignment of tea, amounting to thirty-seven hundredweight, almost two tons.

Some little while earlier, the Sussex smugglers had been expecting to land this tea themselves, without paying duty to the Government, and so making a considerable profit. But the Revenue men had been tipped off, the cutter stationed at Poole had intercepted the vessel carrying the tea, and after a long chase had overhauled her. The illegal cargo had been handed over to the Collector of Customs at Poole and he had put it safely – as he imagined – in his warehouse on the quay.

The smugglers had other ideas. The tea was worth £500, a vast sum in an age when men worked for a few shillings a week. So it was resolved that half the gang should recover the lost cargo while the others picketed the roads leading into Poole and made sure that no troops arrived to interrupt the operation.

The attempt was made on the night of 6 October. The thirty armed smugglers rode into the town about eleven o'clock. They included a particularly ruthless group known as the Hawkhurst gang, led by Thomas Kingsmill and William Fairall.

When they drew near their destination they learned of an unforeseen difficulty: it seemed that there was a sloop moored at the quay, her guns in a position to blast to pieces any crowd of men attacking the Custom House. Some of the party wanted to give up the project, but the Hawkhurst gang declared that if necessary they would do the job alone. While they were still arguing, a man came back and said that the tide was low and the sloop therefore could not bring her cannon to bear on the quay.

There was no more hesitation. The party rode down a back lane to the harbour, left their horses, and crept along the water-front. Then, when the word was given, they battered their way into the warehouse. They were in such numbers, and so well armed, that, whoever they disturbed with their midnight noise, no one risked trying to stop them. The tea was brought out, loaded on to the waiting horses, and spirited away into the darkness.

The next morning the smugglers rode in open triumph through Fordingbridge, weighed out the tea and distributed it in fair shares, and then dispersed.

There were plenty of witnesses, but no one came forward for a long time, despite the reward offered.

One reason was that many honest people resented the taxes which made tea and other commodities so expensive, and were not above buying smuggled goods themselves with no questions asked.

Another reason was fear. Some smugglers might be kindly enough and popular local characters, doing violence to no one, but others spread terror through the countryside and few men dared to give information against them.

No gang was more brutal than the one concerned in that October night affair at Poole.

After some months the King's officers at last found a witness, a Fordingbridge shoemaker named Daniel Chater, who was prepared to give evidence against the smugglers. An elderly customs officer, William Galley, was conducting him to a magistrate when they were seized by a dozen of the gang.

Though the word 'smuggler' may have a romantic sound today, applied to picturesque caves and secret passages, there was nothing pretty about the real thing in the eighteenth century, when smuggling meant big money and encouraged men to stick at nothing.

In this case the two captives might have come to no harm. The smugglers might have kept them hidden somewhere or at most taken them over the Channel and dumped them in France, which was often done when the criminals simply needed time to cover their tracks. In this case it was some of the smugglers' wives who urged their husbands to kill both Chater and his escort.

When darkness fell, the two prisoners were mounted on the same horse, their legs secured with cords passing under its belly, and the gang rode off into the night with them. At every yard the smugglers took turns to lash the helpless men with their whips, until they lost consciousness and slid sideways. Galley they revived and deliberately tortured until he begged them to shoot him. Finally – though it is likely that he was still breathing – they buried him in a sandpit in the woods.

Chater survived two days longer, chained to a post in a hut, while they debated what to do with him. One scheme was to tie a string to the trigger of a gun and all pull together, so that the guilt of his murder would not be borne by any single member of the gang. They rejected this idea as too merciful to the shoemaker.

Instead, after further cruelties, they took him another five miles, tried clumsily and unsuccessfully to hang him, and then threw him head first down a well to die, raining stones upon him so long as they could hear any sound of life.

To destroy every clue, the smugglers even killed Galley's horse, flayed it, and cut the skin into small pieces so that its fate would never be known. Chater's horse was luckier, breaking loose and being eventually restored to its own stable.

For months the disappearance of the two men remained a complete mystery, as the gang had hoped it would. At last came an anonymous letter which led the authorities to Galley's burial place. A second letter gave the name and whereabouts of one of the murderers. He was arrested and turned King's evidence. Seven of the gang, denounced by him, were quickly rounded up and hanged, and in the course of the next few months several more, including Kingsmill and Fairall, ended their brief but bloody careers on the gallows.

They had other crimes on their records, if not on their consciences, and the Hawkhurst gang were by no means the only smugglers who committed murder and appalling tortures. But anyone disposed to feel sentimental about the subject of eighteenth-century smuggling needs only remember the affair of the Poole Custom House and its aftermath.

The Truth About Dick Whittington

'Turn again, Whittington,
Lord Mayor of London!'

That was what Bow bells seemed to be saying to the unhappy boy apprentice in the old story, and the scene has been acted since in a thousand plays and pantomimes.

Many will be surprised to learn that there really *was* a Dick Whittington – but everybody will be sad to think that he probably had no cat to comfort him.

He was certainly Lord Mayor of London, though, and October, when London elected the new Lord Mayor, seems the most appropriate time of year to remember him.

The real Richard Whittington was born at the time of Edward III, the Black Prince, and Chaucer, probably in the early 1360s. We know that he died in March 1423.

He was the third son of a Gloucestershire knight, Sir William Whittington, so he was not a penniless nobody, but like many a younger son of the gentry he had to make his own way in the world by going into business. He went to London and became a mercer, dealing in expensive cloths and materials.

He must have got on well, and made himself popular in the city, for in March 1393, he was made an alderman and quickly afterwards became Sheriff. And when the Lord Mayor, Adam Bamme, died suddenly in June 1397, King Richard II appointed Dick to serve as Lord Mayor until the proper election came round in October, when the votes confirmed the King's choice and Dick was installed Lord Mayor for the following year. They elected

159

him again in 1406 and yet again in 1419, so he was Lord Mayor either three times or four times, according to whether the original term is counted separately.

During these years he prospered in business and the records show that in 1402 he supplied the wedding trousseau for Henry IV's eldest daughter, Blanche, when she married the Duke of Bavaria. In 1405 her sister, Philippa, married Erik, King of Denmark, and it was Dick Whittington to whom she went for her materials.

Actually, the royal family were more obliged to Dick than he to them, for he lent huge sums of money to both Henry IV and Henry V, and the latter's immortal victory at Agincourt was made possible only by the help of Dick and men like him. It was the period of history when merchants and bankers were beginning to play a big part in events, even though they stayed behind the scenes and are not often mentioned. It is easy to remember Dick Whittington, because he has become a storybook character, but he was only one of many rich traders, in London and other cities, who had far more real power than most of the lords and princes in their shining armour.

There is one famous story, very probably true, that Dick gave a banquet to King Henry V and the beautiful French princess, Catherine, he had brought home to be his Queen. Everything was most luxurious and the great crackling fire gave out the fragrance of expensive spices. The smiling Queen remarked on the cost. Dick answered that he would make it even more costly. He pulled out a handful of bills for the money the King owed him – £60,000, the story says – and tossed them into the fire.

If it really happened, one would guess that he had meant to do something similar all along, or he would scarcely have had the documents handy. A cynic might say that he knew he would never be paid, anyhow, and was making the best of it. Warlike kings such as Henry V were often bad payers, but a shrewd businessman found it worth while to lose some money one way in order to gain more another. Raleigh's cloak may have been a similarly crafty move.

By then, too, Dick was nearing the end of his life and had more money than he knew what to do with. He had married Alice long ago – her name at least matches the girl's in the storybooks, though her father, Sir Ivo Fitzwaryn, was a wealthy Dorset knight. But Alice by this time was dead, and they had no children. So, when Dick himself died a few years later, he left everything to charity.

In his old age he had been shocked by the foul conditions in Newgate Prison. Under his will, the place was rebuilt. So was St Bartholomew's Hospital. His money provided a fine floor of Purbeck marble for the new Guildhall, glass windows (quite a luxury, then) with his arms, and half the cost of the Guildhall library, with twenty-eight desks, settles and wainscoting, and a librarian appointed for life. For ordinary townsfolk, who were neither in prison nor hospital nor interested in books, he left money to provide conduits supplying purer drinking water.

Deservedly the Latin words were inscribed on his monument in St Michael's Church, which he had built:

> *Ut fragrans nardus*
> *Fama fuit iste Ricardus,*

meaning:

> Sweet as spikenard
> In repute was this Richard.

It is a pity about the cat. Such stories crop up in many old tales in various countries, but no cat was ever connected with Dick Whittington until many years after his death.

The Secret Passage

Coming-of-age is a time that any boy or girl looks forward to with some sense of excitement. To King Edward III, in the autumn of 1330, his approaching birthday – he would be eighteen on 13 November – was of very special importance.

On that day, if he lived to see it, he would be truly King of England, able to take power into his own hands and no longer the helpless puppet manipulated by others. But would things turn out as simply and straightforwardly as that? Might not something horrible happen before then, as had happened to his own father, the previous King?

That October, living in the great royal fortress at Nottingham, spied on at every turn, Edward felt more like a prisoner than the master of a powerful kingdom.

The real master of England, as everyone knew, was Roger Mortimer, Earl of March. Mortimer held none of the high offices in the government of the country but he controlled it effectively through the lesser men who obeyed his wishes.

Mortimer had reached this position by becoming the lover of Edward's mother, Queen Isabella, whose own ruthless character had won her the nickname of 'the She-Wolf of France'. Her marriage to King Edward II had turned out badly. She had gone home to the French Court, taking her son with her as a small boy, and there she had begun her affair with Mortimer, himself a political fugitive from England. It had been easy then to use the young Prince Edward for their schemes. Just before his fourteenth birthday they had invaded England in his name, deposed his father as unfit to rule, and proclaimed him King. A few months later the captive Edward II had been murdered at Berkeley Castle in Gloucestershire. Mortimer had ordered it and the Queen had not lifted a finger to save her husband.

That much was common gossip throughout the kingdom. So was the scandal of her living with Mortimer. The boy who was now King in name knew all that, but for the moment had to hide his disgust and resentment.

For those four years Mortimer had continued to strengthen his position. He had got rid of enemies and won allies by handing out money and favours. No one could stand against him. With a bodyguard of tough Welsh mercenaries from the hills of his own border country, he overawed all would-be opposition.

Was it likely that he would give up this dominance just because the youth he had placed on the throne became old enough to make his own decisions? Edward was not the only person to be wondering, uncomfortably, what would happen within the next few weeks.

On the eve of his eighteenth birthday the young King felt very much a man. Only that summer, riding in a three-day tournament in London, he had impressed the onlookers with his knightly bearing. For more than two years, indeed, he had been a married man, and this very summer his charming young wife Philippa (later famous as one of the best English Queens) had borne him a son, the future Black Prince. So Edward had every excuse for thinking that his childhood days were behind him.

But would Mortimer agree? Mortimer, who so obviously revelled in the pomp and luxury he would now have to give up?

For this critical period Mortimer had established the court in Nottingham Castle, then one of the principal strongholds in the country, impregnable on its sandstone precipice and ideally placed in the middle of England for a threatened ruler to move in any direction. Every night, the castle keys were ceremonially taken to Queen Isabella's bedchamber. They could hardly be removed from there without Mortimer's knowledge and approval.

So at night Edward was a prisoner within the walls, and during the day he was under constant observation.

Mortimer seemed to hold all the cards in his hand. He was so confident that, at a Council meeting on 19 October, he went too far. He not only abused some of the foremost noblemen present, accusing them of conspiracy against himself, but fired questions at the King.

All the accused lords denied knowledge of any plot. They could hardly do otherwise. But one, William de Montacute, chose his words carefully. He would give a sharp answer, he said with dignity, if he was accused of anything 'inconsistent with his duty'.

Montacute had already made up his mind where duty lay. It was to his King, not to the Earl of March. He took Edward aside after the meeting. 'It would be better,' he said grimly, 'to eat the dog than that the dog eat us.' Edward knew just what he meant, and promptly agreed.

Whether or not there had been a definite plot before, it was now swiftly made. Mortimer must be seized unawares, when his Welshmen were not handy to protect him. But in the daytime that was impossible. And at night Montacute and his friends were lodged in the town outside, cut off from Edward by locked gates and sentries.

How could they get in again, unchallenged? Could it be arranged for the rear gate, the postern, to be left unlocked when the keys were taken to Queen Isabella's bedchamber?

That depended on William d'Eland, deputy constable of the castle. Could he be won over? Only Edward, as his lawful King, could hope to persuade a man of honour in such a responsible position. Edward tackled him. 'On your allegiance,' he murmured ominously. Eland took the point. If he refused, and the King nonetheless succeeded in his plan, he himself would likely hang as a traitor. Eland joined the plot, and suggested a still better scheme.

On the west side, facing away from the town, the Castle Rock rose sheer for a hundred and thirty feet from the deer-park. No armed man could scale that cliff, or the ramparts crowning it, but there was a secret passage, starting at the base of the precipice and coming out in one of the courtyards at the top. This he would reveal to them.

With an opponent like Mortimer there was no time to waste. They acted that same night.

In twos and threes Montacute's supporters, in full armour, slipped away from their lodgings in the town and made their way through the darkness to a certain thicket in the deer-park. Some missed the spot, but a couple of dozen found the rendezvous. There Eland joined them and led them silently to the concealed entrance at the foot of the rock.

A dry sandstone passage curved upwards, sometimes with rough-hewn steps. At last they came out into the fresh October air again. Edward stepped out of the shadows and greeted them mutely. It was late. Most of the Castle's occupants were asleep. Any watchmen were not expecting intruders to emerge from the bowels of the earth.

Mortimer, however, had not yet gone to bed. He was in the room next to the Queen's bedchamber, consulting with the Lord Chancellor and other close supporters.

At the last moment, too late, the alarm was given. An usher

shouted a warning just as the party reached the door. A steward, Hugh de Turpington, one of Isabella's loyal retainers, drew his dagger and rushed at them, shouting: 'Down with the traitors!' One of the party, John de Neville, cut him down. A second man, Richard de Monmouth, tried to bar their way. He too was killed. The King's men swept through the door and overpowered Mortimer and his companions. Isabella rushed in from her chamber, distractedly, pleading: 'Have pity on the gentle Mortimer!' but the word 'gentle' rang oddly in the ears of men who suspected the atrocity with which Mortimer had put the late King to death. Edward ignored his mother's cry. He ordered Mortimer to be fettered and sent to London.

That October night was, in effect, the beginning of Edward III's long and eventful reign which lasted another forty-seven years, covering Crécy, Poitiers, the Black Death, and much else that was to figure in the history-books. Mortimer was executed as a traitor. Isabella was allowed to live out her life in honourable and comfortable retirement, but she never had any political influence again.

As for the secret passage, it is still known as 'Mortimer's Hole', and for a few pence the modern visitor to Nottingham Castle can descend it with a guide.

November

A Superior Lady's Maid

Her parents had given way at last. On 25 November 1773, a dark-eyed, black-haired girl of eighteen walked up the aisle of Holy Trinity Church in Coventry – an old building fortunately spared by the bombs that destroyed the cathedral next to it in a later November 1940. At her side walked her father, with all the poise and dignity of an experienced actor-manager, masking his disapproval as well as he could.

A little while later the bride signed her name for the last time as Sarah Kemble. Henceforth she was Mrs Siddons, and under that new name she was destined to become one of the most famous actresses in the annals of the theatre.

There had been plenty of drama, off stage as well as on, before that November wedding in Coventry.

Sarah was the eldest of the twelve Kemble children. From babyhood, apart from spells at various private schools, she had shared the travelling life of her parents. They toured the West Midland and Welsh Border towns, playing a few nights here and a few nights there, or even one-night stands, in the assembly rooms, inns and barns of the district, before heaping their costume-boxes, curtains and scenery into their wagon and driving on again over the bumpy rutted tracks that passed for roads in Georgian England. Proper theatre buildings were very few.

To save wages for other actors, the Kemble children were cast for small parts as soon as they were old enough. Sarah was twelve when she played Princess Elizabeth in *Charles the First* at Worcester.

In the play was a young man named William Siddons in the role of Duke of Richmond. William was not a very good actor, but Sarah found other qualities in him to admire. During the next few years, as she grew into her teens and acted regularly with the company, the young couple fell in love.

Mr and Mrs Kemble were not having that. They had bigger ideas for their daughter. Her beauty was attracting notice wherever she appeared. At Brecon the local squire had heard her sing 'Robin, sweet Robin' and the combination of her voice and looks had swept him off his feet. If she did not marry Mr Evans, there were plenty of other young gentlemen paying court to her. Though touring stage-folk were usually looked down upon, as little better than the 'rogues and vagabonds' they had once been, Sarah had such refinement that, with her intelligence and lovely appearance, she could take her place in any class of society.

Her parents tried to break up her friendship with William. When they could not, they gave him notice to leave the company.

It was usual for departing members to be given a benefit night. This farewell performance took place in Brecon, where Sarah had been born at the Shoulder of Mutton Inn during an earlier tour. It was also usual, at the fall of the curtain, for the actor in question to make a speech of thanks and farewell. This was often prepared in rhymed verse.

On this occasion William Siddons duly stepped forward and recited eleven doggerel verses which he had rather pointedly entitled 'The Discarded Lover'. The verses informed the goggling audience how shabbily he had been treated by his employers.

As he bowed to the applause and made a graceful exit, Mrs Kemble – a woman of strong personality and temperament – met him in the wings and boxed his ears.

She had not, however, seen the last of William.

Sarah refused to forget her lover. She would not marry Squire Evans or anyone else. Yet at seventeen, as the law then stood, she must wait another four years before she could defy her parents' wishes and choose her own husband. What were the Kembles to do? They could not imprison her, like a fairy-tale princess, in some inaccessible tower. But they hit upon a solution that came very near to it.

There stood – and still stands – just outside Warwick a country mansion, then newly built, romantically perched on a rocky tree-clad bluff rising from a broad, placid expanse of the River Avon. It is called Guy's Cliff and stands on medieval foundations.

In 1771 the house was the home of a young widow, Lady Mary Greatheed, daughter of the Duke of Ancaster. It was arranged that Sarah should go there as a lady's maid and companion. Guy's Cliff, now a favourite Warwickshire beauty-spot, admired across the river by countless motorists and walkers, was then an isolated spot. The girl would be safe there, and, as William was a poor man, hampered by the need to earn his living on tour with another company, the Kembles saw little danger of his turning up to resume his wooing.

They were mistaken in this. Not only did Sarah manage to keep up a correspondence with her lover but they were able to meet on occasions when he passed through the district.

Lady Mary was a very human person, good-natured and without that overweening sense of her own importance that so often went with noble rank in those days. She was charmed with Sarah and treated her well. In essence she felt the girl was as much a 'lady' as she was herself. Thanks to her schooling and her stage experience, Sarah's voice and deportment were strikingly good. As Lady Mary was to confess laughingly in after years, she often had to check an impulse to rise when Sarah came into a room. It was Sarah who, quite naturally and unaffectedly, brought with her the aura of aristocratic dignity.

When she went with Lady Mary to visit her mother, the Duchess, at the great house in Lincolnshire, Sarah had to drop into the background somewhat. Now, instead of being her mistress's continual companion, she must take her meals in the servants' hall.

There was no great hardship in this. The servants of a ducal household lived well and had their own grades of importance – Sarah's status made her an honoured guest at the top table with the butler, the cook, and other senior members of the staff. Very soon her beauty and dramatic talents made her popular as well as respected. The servants found that she could act, and, once they saw how superbly she performed, she was made to go through all her repertoire and to repeat the most favoured items over and over again.

It is hard now to imagine Sarah's impact on the servants' hall at Ancaster in those days when television, radio and cinema were still unknown. Those maids and footmen could not realize that they were being entertained by one who would be recognized in a few years as 'the incomparable Siddons' and the queen of tragedy in the English theatre. They knew only that they were being splendidly, unforgettably entertained. Never had the off-duty hours in that great household flown by with such excitement and delight.

A rumour of what was going on drifted upstairs and reached the ears of Lady Mary's brother. Lord Robert went down and slipped into the audience. When he returned to the drawing-room he was full of enthusiasm.

Be careful, his sister begged. Sarah's parents did not want her to follow them on the stage. The life was too hard. Two of her sisters were to become a milliner and a dressmaker respectively.

Sarah was not to be encouraged in any theatrical ambitions. Reading poetry was all right – Lady Mary had herself given Sarah a copy of Milton's works – but play-acting was not to be encouraged.

Lady Mary and the Kembles could have spared themselves the effort of opposition. Sarah followed the path along which her strong nature drove her. She was determined to make her career as an actress – and she was determined to have her William.

Her parents gave up the hopeless struggle. In November 1773, the wedding took place at Coventry, the young couple were received back into Mr Kemble's Company of Comedians, and the immortal name of 'Sarah Siddons' appeared for the first time on the play-bills.

It is pleasant to know that, years afterwards, Lady Mary Greatheed welcomed Sarah as an old friend and honoured guest at Guy's Cliff, the house where she had once been a superior lady's maid.

Gunpowder Plot

'Remember, remember, the fifth of November,' runs the old rhyme. Yet how much does anyone now remember of that famous event which never came off? A man named Guy Fawkes tried to blow up Parliament... With that single fact most people's knowledge of the affair abruptly stops.

Poor Fawkes, who is still burned yearly in effigy on countless bonfires, was really only a secondary character in a long mystery story which had opened more than two years earlier.

The real villain of the piece – or hero, as some believed – was a young Warwickshire gentleman, Robert Catesby. Six feet tall, handsome, with fascinating manners and a magnetic personality, Catesby was courageous but over-impulsive. A zealous Roman Catholic, he had been in trouble more than once during the last years of Queen Elizabeth's reign. When James I became king – an event by no means popular with everyone in England – Catesby's dream of a revolution became an obsession.

Within two months, as early as May 1603, he was discussing with intimate friends a plan to kill James. By January 1604, he had formulated a scheme to blow up the Parliament house when the King was in it.

These dates are important. When James had first come south from Scotland to take over his inherited kingdom he had declared his intention to be more tolerant of his Roman Catholic subjects than the previous regime had been. They were to be free to worship God according to their consciences. So Catesby's project was not provoked by repression. It was only when careless talk began to spread rumours of Catholic plots that James's government brought back, in 1604 and 1605, the only penalties and restrictions imposed on followers of 'the old religion'. Even so, most moderate Catholics were quite prepared to live under the existing laws of England. Only the extremists like Catesby believed in revolt.

Guy Fawkes enters the story in April 1604. A tall Yorkshireman, with brown hair and an auburn beard, he was like Catesby in his early thirties. Born a Protestant, he had been converted, and like many converts was therefore all the more zealous in his religion. He had gone abroad and served gallantly with the Spanish army in Flanders, and it was from Flanders that the conspirators now brought him back to England. Unlike Catesby, Fawkes was a mild and temperate man, never one to mix in broils and troubles if they could be avoided.

On 24 May the plan went another step forward. One of Catesby's associates, Thomas Percy, was able to rent a house in Westminster next door to the Parliament building, which

Catesby had marked out as the ideal spot for catching the King and his ministers at the same time.

The plot, however, proceeded with incredible slowness. There was much to be arranged. There was no point in merely destroying the Government unless preparations were complete for the seizing of power and for friendly intervention from abroad. Many people had to be sounded out in secret, many bargains struck.

It was not until 11 December that tunnelling began from the cellar of the rented house to the vaults underlying the House of Lords. Progress was so desultory that by March 1605, the conspirators were only half-way through. Then – and here a little humour brightens the dark story – they found that they could have saved their trouble, for Percy was able to rent the very vault they were tunnelling to reach, right beneath the Chamber in which Lords and Commons would assemble for the opening of Parliament by the King.

Into this vault they smuggled more than a ton and a half of gunpowder. Guy Fawkes supervised the operation as the experienced soldier. Besides camouflaging the explosive with heaps of coal and firewood, he laid iron bars on the top to increase the lethal effect.

The conspirators had still to wait until the autumn, 5 November to be precise, but the interval gave them more time to perfect their other plans.

It was assumed that the Prince of Wales, the boy Henry, would be standing beside his father and would perish with him in the explosion. His younger brother (the future Charles I) and his sister, Elizabeth, would be elsewhere. They must be kidnapped, so that any surviving members of the Government could not use them as figure-heads to rally the people against the revolutionaries. Various conspirators were to be entrusted with these duties. Guy Fawkes, being the man with contacts overseas, was to flee abroad as soon as he had set off the explosion, and organize foreign support.

There was one snag fated to ruin everything.

Many innocent individuals, including some devout Roman

Catholic peers, were likely to be killed or hideously injured when all that gunpowder went off under their feet. Some of the conspirators were more squeamish than Catesby, who was so fanatical that he was ready to sacrifice friends as well as enemies for the sake of his cause. Catesby was adamant that no one should be warned to stay away.

Some details of the affair remain wrapped in mystery, historians still argue hotly about them, and the complete truth will never now be known. But it seems likely that Catesby's cousin, Francis Tresham, was acutely concerned for his brother-in-law, Lord Monteagle, and warned him. Though Monteagle was himself a Catholic sympathizer, he insisted that the massacre must be prevented. It must be done, though, in such a way that the plotters had time to escape.

The next move, a few days later on 26 October, was odd indeed. Lord Monteagle opened up a house he had not occupied for the past year. Some unknown – who but Tresham? – must have known he would be taking supper there, for an unsigned letter was delivered to him at the table. No less oddly, Monteagle passed it to a gentleman named Ward, whom he knew to be a close friend of Robert Winter, a prominent conspirator. Ward read it aloud. No names were mentioned and there was no reference to the vault or its gunpowder. Monteagle was merely warned to stay away from Parliament and avoid 'a terrible blow'. He was to burn the letter.

He did not, and he was not meant to. Instead he hastened to Whitehall to warn the Secretary of State, Robert Cecil, now Lord Salisbury and known as 'the crook-backed earl'. As he went, Monteagle knew he could rely on Ward to warn Winter that the secret was out.

Now, however, events did not follow their expected course. Having only the vague warning in the letter, even the shrewd Salisbury could take no immediate action. And the conspirators, finding that no move was made against them, recovered their nerve and stood firm. Fawkes confirmed that no one had been near the cellar and that the gunpowder was undisturbed.

November arrived. Peers and M.P.s streamed into London for the opening of Parliament. Fawkes took up his position, armed with a slow match that would give him a quarter of an hour to escape before it ignited the powder.

On 4 November King James was shown the warning letter. James had a nose for danger – all his life he had lived in fear of assassination – and he told the Lord Chamberlain to search the building. Fawkes was discovered in the vault, but his thirty-six barrels of gunpowder remained unnoticed, and he was simply asked who owned the great mound of coal and faggots. He answered truthfully, 'Thomas Percy', for the place was rented in that name, and the searchers went away.

But the name 'Thomas Percy' aroused suspicion, and within a few hours a magistrate arrived with another search-party, uncovered the gunpowder and arrested Fawkes. He was taken off to the King's bedchamber at one o'clock in the morning, where, face to face with James, he defiantly admitted his intention to 'blow back the Scots into Scotland'. But even under the cruellest torture he would not betray the names of his confederates until, by 9 November, they were all killed or captured.

Catesby and Percy were shot in Staffordshire, where the country house in which they had taken refuge was stormed by the sheriff and his men. Fawkes, Winter, and six others died on the gallows, and Frencis Tresham in a dungeon in the Tower.

For generations afterwards – as long as religion remained a violent issue in English politics – 5 November remained, with its bonfires and fireworks and 'guys', an anniversary fraught with propagandist significance, not just a rather dangerous children's festivity.

Grand Tourists in Trouble

'So, as the song says, we are in fair Italy!' wrote young Horace Walpole to a former school friend on 11 November 1739. 'I wonder we are,' he added, and proceeded to describe his adventures in crossing the snow-clad Alpine passes with his companion, the poet Thomas Gray.

They had been four days in the mountains. At the foot of Mont Cenis their chaise had been dismantled and loaded, piece by piece, on mules. They themselves, 'swathed in beaver bonnets, beaver gloves, beaver stockings, muffs, and bear-skins', were 'carried in low arm-chairs on poles' by local bearers who specialized in this service to travellers.

Walpole was an elegant, witty youth, polished at Eton and Cambridge, the son of Robert Walpole, George II's famous Prime Minister. He admired the 'dexterity and nimbleness of the mountaineers', who 'run with you down steeps and frozen precipices where no man, as men are now, could possibly walk', but he was understandably unnerved when these 'Alpine savages' began quarrelling among themselves at one of the dizziest points of the journey. Gray's porters shoved their way past his own where 'the least slip had tumbled us into such a fog, and such an eternity, as we should never have found our way out of again', while the two young Englishmen sat helpless in their swaying chairs.

Luckily they survived the experience, Gray to write his famous *Elegy* and other poems, Walpole to delight subsequent generations with some of the most amusing letters in literature. The purpose of this foreign journey was to make the 'Grand Tour' to Italy, then considered essential to every young English gentleman's education.

A War Correspondent with a Future

The armoured train, puffing gallantly across the South African veld, was disrespectfully known as 'Wilson's Deathtrap'. Its makeshift armour was a doubtful defence against the fire of the Boers, but the young war correspondent travelling in it knew that it was safer than sitting on a horse with no protection at all.

He had good reason to know. At twenty-four he had been under fire in a Cuban revolution, served with the Bengal Lancers against the Afghans, and taken part at Omdurman in the last full-scale cavalry charge in history.

Now, in 1899, as Queen Victoria's long reign drew near its close, he had hurried out to South Africa to report on the war that had flared up against the independent republics of the Dutch-speaking settlers, the Boers.

The British forces in Ladysmith were besieged. The relieving army used the train for daily reconnaissance up and down the line, as near as it could get to the beleaguered town. On 15 November the young journalist went with it.

It was an enterprising idea, but it turned out to be unlucky. The train entered a cutting and at once came under fire from Boers on either side, using field-guns as well as their deadly rifles.

It looked as though 'Wilson's Deathtrap' was well named. The train could not go forward, nor could it go back, for the last three trucks had come off the rails. The soldiers on board, men of the Dublin Fusiliers and a local unit, the Durban Light Infantry, were caught.

It was the journalist who rose to the emergency. Strictly, as a civilian, he had no right to intervene. But his past training as a British cavalry officer, together with his naturally aggressive spirit, made it impossible for him to do nothing.

He leapt down on to the track and organized some of the men into a breakdown gang. Luckily the engine was always placed in the middle of the train as a precaution. He had it un-coupled and run backwards, time and again, as a battering-ram to knock the derailed trucks out of the way. And all the time the Boer shots were whistling about his ears.

At last the track behind them was clear once more. But it was impossible to couple the locomotive to the forward half of the train again and haul it to safety. All that could be done was to pack the wounded into the cab and send the engine back by itself. The others had to surrender.

The journalist was alarmed when he was separated from the soldiers. He thought the Boers meant to shoot him as a non-combatant who had wrongly joined in the fight. But the Boers had read the name on his papers, 'Winston Churchill', and meant to keep him as a prisoner of special value. They could not foresee that one day he would be Prime Minister of Britain and one of the world's outstanding statesmen. What impressed them was that he was the cousin of the Duke of Marlborough.

They did not hold him for long. The man who forty years later was to defy Hitler did not intend to sit meekly as a prisoner. Within a few weeks he made his escape.

First he hid beneath some sacks in a train. Then he spent three days at the bottom of a coal-mine with only rats for company. Then the mine-manager, an Englishman named John Howard, smuggled him back to the surface and gave him a more comfortable hiding-place behind some wooden cases in his office. There he could while away the boredom with a copy of Stevenson's *Kidnapped*.

A Boer patrol came to the mine. There was a reward of £25 for Winston Churchill, dead or alive. Even allowing for the greater value of money in those days, it was rather less than the Nazis would have offered in 1940. But John Howard had distracted the Boers' attention and they had not set foot in his office.

The same night there was a goods train carrying wool across the border into Portuguese East Africa, neutral territory where the fugitive would be safe. Churchill travelled on it, crouching in a tiny space among the bales of wool, and an adventure which had started with one kind of train finished with another.

Flight of a Princess

For the young Princess Anne (later to rule as Queen) November 1688 was probably the most exciting month in her life.

That month brought the so-called 'Glorious Revolution', anxiously awaited but delayed by the winds of October making it impossible for William of Orange to sail across from Holland.

The English nation was racked with furious political disagreement, and the princess found herself unwillingly involved at the centre of it.

She was pulled one way by natural obedience to her father, James II. On the other hand, she felt strong sympathy with her elder sister, Mary, married to their Dutch cousin, William, ruler of the Netherlands.

Religion lay at the root of the trouble. The two sisters, like the majority of the English people – and the Dutch, were Protestants. James, however, was a zealous Roman Catholic. Since becoming King three years ago, he had more and more alarmed his subjects with fears that he would take away the freedoms they had won. In the seventeenth century a man's faith was not his private business but affected his career and almost every important aspect of his life.

After the failure of the amateurish Monmouth Rebellion the

Protestants had tried to be patient. James would not live for ever. When he died, the crown would go to Mary, or failing her to Anne, and the country would have a Church of England monarch again. But in June 1688 that comforting hope was destroyed: the King's second wife, an Italian Catholic, bore him a son who would now come before Mary and Anne as heir to the throne – and would obviously be brought up in his parents' beliefs.

Desperate, the Protestants persuaded themselves that this baby (later known to history as 'the Old Pretender') was not of royal birth but a changeling, smuggled into the palace by a political trick. Few people believe this story now, but many did at the time. Anne was away in Bath when the baby arrived. She accepted the Protestant propaganda. So did her sister in Holland. Both felt that their father and stepmother were deceiving them.

When William of Orange landed at Torbay in Devon, on 5 November, heading a well-equipped army of volunteers to 'maintain the Protestant religion and the liberties of England', Anne knew that she would soon have to reveal where her first loyalty lay.

She was at this date twenty-three, a not particularly clever young woman, fond of stag-hunting, horse-racing (it was she who later founded the Ascot meeting) and playing cards. She was married to a very dull Dane, Prince George, who drank too much but was none the livelier for it. As the previous King, Charles II, had complained, 'I've tried him drunk and I've tried him sober, but 'od's fish, there's nothing in him.' They had had three children already, but none had lived long.

Prince George had gone off with the King, still outwardly loyal to him, to join the army concentrating at Salisbury to meet William's forces advancing from the west. Anne knew that, when the right moment came, her husband would desert to William. So would the husband of her closest friend, Sarah Churchill. Indeed, the King's desertion by John Churchill (the future Duke of Marlborough and ancestor of Winston) would be one of the factors costing James his crown.

While their husbands rode to war with these secret intentions in their hearts, Anne and Sarah waited anxiously in London. Anne had quarters in the Cockpit, part of the vast rambling palace of Whitehall which was not one building but more like a village of separate apartments and halls.

At last, on 25 November, came the news that Prince George had escaped from the royal camp to join William. That evening, the Queen came storming over to Anne's quarters, taxed her step-daughter with treachery, and even (it is said) struck her in the face. When she had flounced out, Anne decided it was time for her too to go. She knew that Sarah Churchill's arrest was ordered for the next morning, and she herself, though the King's daughter, might not be safe.

She had a staunch friend in Dr Compton, Bishop of London, who was under suspension for his defiance of the King. Compton had been Anne's tutor as a girl, he had performed her wedding ceremony, and she trusted him as an old friend. Also, in his dashing youth, Compton had been a cavalry officer, so in a crisis like this he was ready, in his own words, to 'lay aside the Bible

at present' and get out his sword and pistols again. He was just the man to help Anne and Sarah escape.

Anne went to bed, telling her servants not to disturb her next morning until she rang. After midnight she crept down the back stairs with Sarah, another officer's wife, and one maid. They walked a short way through the darkness and found Dr Compton waiting with a coach.

They spent the rest of that night hidden at his house. Then, at first light, they took the road northwards, away from the possible battle-ground of the West Country, heading for Nottingham where William's supporters had seized the castle.

Compton rode beside the coach, his sword drawn, his pistols loaded in their holsters, enjoying every minute of the adventure.

Within a few days the King's cause had collapsed and Anne was driving triumphantly south again. Her father fled abroad into exile. Some months later Anne saw her sister crowned, with William as joint sovereign, in Westminster Abbey. And it was Bishop Compton who performed the ceremony.

December

'Next to Godliness'

'On the vigil of Thomas the apostle,' ordered Lanfranc, who became Archbishop of Canterbury, in 1070, 'the brethren shall be shaved and let those who will take a bath, in such wise that all shall have taken it two days before Christmas Day.' This gave the monks three days in which to share out the hot water, and Lanfranc was strict in his instructions.

'Let the bathing be ordered as follows,' he went on. The abbot was to appoint a 'devout and prudent senior' who would supervise and provide suitable bath attendants, 'mature men, neither children nor youths', and if saw 'anything unfitting' he was to tell the chamberlain. As a safeguard against larking about or other mis-behaviour, 'let him take care that the youths and novices go not all together, but with their elders'.

When their turn came, each party was to proceed to the bath, their change of clean clothing in their hands, and then undress, 'and letting down the curtain that hangs before them they shall sit in silence in the bath'. If a monk needed anything he was not to call out but to 'signal for it quietly, and a servant lifting the veil shall quickly take him what he wants'. When he had finished washing himself the monk was not to 'stay longer for pleasure' but dry himself, dress and return to the cloister.

One was not encouraged to enjoy baths. 'Let baths be granted to the sick as often as it shall be expedient,' St Benedict had laid down long ago, 'but to those in health, and especially to the young, they shall be seldom permitted.'

Archbishop Lanfranc thought that five hot baths a year were a reasonable allowance, clean clothes being put on at the same time. As the monks slept in their clothes, and washed only their face and hands on ordinary days, the odour of sanctity must have been noticeable by 20 December when the fifth and last bath of the year became due.

On the whole, however, monks were cleaner than the medieval man in the street. Only the upper classes bathed oftener. King John took a bath every three weeks – but then John was a byword for luxury and self-indulgence.

A Merry Christmas in Wales

The Christmas of 1215 saw more merriment in Wales than there had been for many a long year. Throughout December the warrior prince, Llewelyn ap Iorwerth – 'Llewelyn the Great', as he is now remembered – had been sweeping through the country with his men. One by one the Norman castles had opened their gates to him, and finally, on 26 December, the fortress of Cardigan gave in.

'The Welsh,' wrote the chronicler, 'returned joyfully to their homes, but the French, driven out of all their holds, wandered hither and thither like birds in melancholy wise.'

The 'French' were the Anglo-Norman lords who for more than a century had been gradually pushing their way into the country, taking over the fertile valleys and establishing themselves along the coast. There were Flemish colonists, too, settled in the southwestern tip in Pembrokeshire. More and more the Welsh had been driven into the hills. They were a poor people, unable to match the mail-clad knights of the King of England in set battles.

Llewelyn's triumph, that Christmas, was the end of a struggle

he had waged for some years against King John. To understand his achievement one must look back to his boyhood.

He was born into the princely family that ruled Gwynedd, North Wales that is, including the craggy Snowdon ranges and the corn-growing off-shore island of Anglesey. To gain the leadership his father had once held before him, the boy was forced to assert himself against his uncles, playing off one relative against another. By 1201, when King John had recently succeeded Richard Lionheart on the English throne, Llewelyn was acknowledged as the foremost man in Wales.

He wanted to keep his people free, but he knew that he must go carefully. His neighbour, England, was too big to destroy. England would not go away, or sink beneath the sea. He must try to make friends with John. He would even bow to John, personally, as his overlord, provided that John did not try to take away the liberties of Wales.

To strengthen their friendship, he took John's daughter Joan as his wife, and the marriage seems to have been happy.

The King, however, proved no friend to his son-in-law. He continued to extend the English power in Wales. He marched arrogantly through South Wales with a host of tough mercenaries and a column of siege-engines that could batter down any wall. He occupied Cardigan Castle, always known as 'the key to Wales', and many other strongholds. The Welsh had only one special asset in battle – they were the first to develop the longbow into a powerful armour-piercing weapon. Though it later became a famous English weapon, associated with Robin Hood and the victory of Crécy, it originated in South Wales. It helped the Welsh to wage guerrilla warfare, but they could not win by archery alone.

Llewelyn resisted John in the north, but he was driven back into the barren hills of Snowdonia, where his men would have been starved out if Joan had not ridden down to plead with her father. John spared Llewelyn but on harsh terms. He must surrender half the land of Gwynedd, along with twenty thousand cattle, numerous horses and other stock, and thirty hostages as a guarantee that he would keep his word.

John had a ruthless way with hostages. Some time later, when his continued encroachments in Wales had driven the people to revolt again, he gathered his forces at Nottingham Castle in September 1212, to march against the Welsh – and on that occasion he was in such a fury that he would not sit down to dinner until a number of the hostages had been hanged from the battlements.

Llewelyn bided his time. At Easter 1214, John summoned him to court at Cambridge. He dared not refuse. But during the Easter celebrations, mixing with the English barons and keeping his ears cocked for the murmurings behind the King's back, he realized how many enemies the King had in England as well as in Wales.

The next year came the revolt of the barons which forced John to agree to Magna Carta at Runnymede on 15 June 1215. In that movement the Welsh prince made common cause with the lords of England. Three clauses were included in the document, relating to Wales: all hostages were to be returned, Welshmen deprived of their land were to get it back, and all disputes in Wales were to be settled by Welsh law.

John did not keep his word as soon as he had got safely away from Runnymede. Within months he had involved himself in civil war with his barons, who called in the French king to aid them. This confused situation gave Llewelyn his chance. It was then that he raised the standard of revolt in Wales and carried all before him.

The death of John, the next year, leaving a boy of nine to take the English throne as Henry III, meant that Llewelyn had time to establish his power in Wales. Later, when trouble came again, his wife made more than one journey to the court of her young half-brother in England and helped to keep the peace between them. So, by his own wisdom and Joan's aid, Llewelyn secured Welsh freedom for the rest of his life. Towards the end, having suffered a stroke, he gave up his power to their son, David. He retired to a Cistercian monastery at Strata Florida, a beautiful spot in Cardiganshire such as those monks loved to choose for their abbeys. There, in the quiet hills beside the River Teifi, he died in 1240, twenty-five years after that crowning Christmas victory at Cardigan.

A Crown for the Conqueror

'And William conquered this land,' wrote the Saxon monk in the cloisters at Peterborough, carefully forming the black letters on the parchment of his chronicle, 'and he came to Westminster, and Archbishop Ealdred consecrated him King . . .'.

He was too tactful to mention that Ealdred was Archbishop of York, and that the Archbishop of Canterbury, who should really have performed the ceremony, had declined to do so.

It was easier for William of Newburgh, a Yorkshire churchman living a hundred years later, to write frankly. 'Stigand, Archbishop of Canterbury,' he recorded, 'refused to "lay hands" on one who, as he alleged, was a bloody man, and the invader of another's rights. However, Ealdred, Archbishop of York, a good and wise man, discharged this function, realizing, more astutely, that one should yield to the times, and not resist the dispensation of Providence.'

Stigand's career did not prosper after this, and though the new King took no immediate steps against him he soon lost his position and died in prison five years later.

His attitude over the coronation must have infuriated the strong-willed Norman. Though William had won the Battle of Hastings and his rival, Harold, was dead, he was very anxious to appear as the lawful King of England, not merely as one who had conquered the country by force. So it was most important that all the usual forms should be observed and that he should be crowned with exactly the same ceremonies as all the kings before him, as far back as anyone could remember.

The coronation was fixed for 'Midwinter Day', that is, Christmas

Day, 1066. It would take place in the church of the great new Benedictine abbey at Westminster, which had been completed and consecrated just before the death of King Edward the Confessor, a year earlier. It stood outside London, a mile upstream, but already quite a township had grown up around it. Edward had often lived there, so that he could keep an eye on the building which was so dear to his heart. He meant it to be the church for all future coronations and he gave its monks the privilege of guarding the regalia.

Even at that early date, the coronation was an ancient institution. Ceremonies such as the anointing with holy oil had been performed at every crowning for the past three hundred years. At first it had been a helmet that had been placed on the royal head. A crown, a ring and a sword had been introduced into the service later.

William had ordered a new crown, more splendid than the one Harold is shown wearing in the Bayeux Tapestry. It was made by a Byzantine goldsmith, using gold sent from Arabia and gems from Egypt – though obviously there could not have been time to send to Arabia and Egypt for the materials *after* his triumph at Hastings. Guy of Amiens described this crown as 'a miracle of splendour' and listed all the separate jewels, topaz, sapphire, emerald and the rest, and the pearl on the top which stood supreme and 'refilled the stones with added light'.

William was then a fit figure to wear it. Still under forty, he was tall and powerfully built, handsome in a stern way, though able to charm with a smile when he wished.

As the crown was placed on his dark, short-cropped head, the great church echoed thunderously with the cries of acclamation, '*Vivat! Vivat!*' customary at this most significant moment in the service.

The Norman men-at-arms on guard outside heard this tumult within. Not having been briefed with every detail in the programme – which was English and unfamiliar to them – they jumped to the conclusion that treachery was afoot and that their Duke was being attacked. While some rushed in to the rescue, others fell upon the crowd outside. Panic ensued. The rumour was easily started but not so easily stopped. By the time that order was restored, and the angry Norman soldiers assured that their leader was safe, they had already set fire to many of the buildings standing round the Abbey. As the Westminster of those days was a place of largely timber houses, with thatched roofs, the township was quickly in flames.

Altogether it was a coronation, and a Christmas, that nobody was likely to forget.

The Mysterious Duke

On 6 December 1879, died William John Cavendish Bentinck-Scott, fifth Duke of Portland, one of the most mysterious and eccentric characters ever to be numbered among the English nobility. That is saying a great deal, for the noblemen of England have included more than their fair share of human oddities.

The dead Duke had played no important part in the history of Victorian times. Indeed no one but his own discreet and tight-lipped servants had seen his face for a long time. He was unmarried. For the twenty-five years he had been Duke, he had lived as a recluse on his vast country estate at Welbeck Abbey, in Sherwood Forest. When he travelled to London his carriage was made fast on a flat railway truck at the rear of the train and he sat in it, with the green silk blinds drawn down over the windows, throughout the journey. His town residence, Harcourt House, had high screens of frosted glass all round the garden, so that, without loss of sunshine, it was hidden from outside observers.

It was not difficult in the nineteenth century for a man to indulge in the oddest whims if he had the money to pay for them.

If he had a title, it was easier still. So the Duke could do exactly as he pleased, and never lack staff or other people to meet his requirements without question.

There was no doubt about the money, as the new Duke and his family quickly found.

Since the old man had died a bachelor of seventy-nine, the title and estates fell to his twenty-one-year-old cousin, orphaned son of an army general, who had been living in modest circumstances with his widowed stepmother, three schoolboy brothers, and little half-sister, Ottoline. Ottoline was only six, but from her vivid recollections, published long afterwards, the excitement of that December can be recreated.

She was taken up to London to stay at Claridge's exclusive hotel. White wooden boxes arrived from the hot-houses at Welbeck, filled with luscious grapes and peaches nestling in pink paper. She and her youngest half-brother were taken to a famous toyshop in Regent Street and allowed to choose whatever toys they liked. 'After our comparative poverty,' she recalled, 'this seemed like Fairyland. I chose a doll dressed in spangled blue satin.' Soon it was explained to her that, though her father had just missed becoming Duke himself, by dying just before his cousin, she and the younger boys would have titles as Duke's children, and henceforth she would be called 'Lady Ottoline'.

At the end of December the whole family set off for Nottinghamshire, to see the ancestral home in which none of them had ever set foot. It was a dark, windy night when they got out of the train at Worksop, and a little crowd of sightseers had gathered in the pallid light of the station oil-lamps. Two carriages were waiting outside. They climbed in – Ottoline's beautiful mother with her raven-black hair, the big brother they were already learning to call 'Portland', then Henry and Bill and Charlie, and Ottoline with her nurse, Powell. Then off they drove for miles through the night.

After the weary journey the arrival was at first a shocking disappointment. They had heard that the old Duke had cared for nothing but building strange underground tunnels, but they had hardly expected to find the drive such a morass of builders' rubbish that they could reach the front door only across a temporary causeway of planks. Inside, it was just as bad. There was no floor to the hall. They had to pick their way across it on more planks. Respectful figures loomed out of the lamplight, a tall Scottish steward and other senior servants. With murmured apologies they led the family to the west wing, which contained the few usable rooms in all that vast mansion.

In the morning the young people set out to explore. Their own rooms opened one into another and, though the Duke had lived in them, were shabbily furnished. The door of the suite had two letter-boxes, one each side, so that the Duke's outgoing mail could also be passed through without opening the door. A servant explained that fires had been kept up all night in every room, for His Grace was quite likely to get up in the small hours, take a bath, and finish the night in a different bed.

Venturing further, the children found that the rest of the house was practically without furniture. All the rooms were decorated in pink, with gilding in the main apartments. To Ottoline's startled eyes it seemed that almost every room possessed just a single seat – a water-closet, in full working order, stood in one corner, shameless and unscreened.

Then they came to the famous underground passages which had been the Duke's great enthusiasm. They followed one and came up through a trap-door into what had been a riding-school in Cavalier times, but had been filled now with innumerable mirrors, crystal chandeliers, and stacks of oil paintings.

A second passage led to the kitchens. The late Duke had been liable to demand roast chicken at any hour, and expected one to be ready within a moment. The cook had taken care always to have a chicken turning on the spit at all times. Presumably, in that huge establishment, there was always someone glad enough to consume the innumerable birds that never reached the ducal table. But when an order did arrive from His Grace, the hot dishes were swiftly sent down by lift, transferred to a heated trolley running on rails, and pushed underground to the main buildings of the Abbey.

There were many other such passages – the Duke's 'walking tunnel' to the gardens, nearly a mile away, a parallel but rougher tunnel for the menial staff, and the even longer 'driving tunnel' wide enough for two carriages to pass. This one actually went beneath the lake, and for that stretch was lit by gas. There were also three vast subterranean apartments, painted the Duke's favourite pink, gas-lit, parquet-floored, and warmed by hot air. But none were furnished, none used.

What was the answer to the riddle? Had the late Duke been mad? Had he been a leper, or victim of some other monstrous disfigurement, that he never showed his face to the outside world?

Ottoline and her brothers had heard the strange stories, but they learnt nothing at Welbeck to confirm them.

The Duke, said his old servants, had been a tall, extremely handsome man, not unlike the great Duke of Wellington, though with a harsher expression. He had been a strict master, but with odd quirks of kindness. He had employed hundreds of workmen to excavate his underground passages, and he had provided them with donkeys to ride to work and with big umbrellas for wet weather. He had provided a big skating-rink for the use of his staff, with dozens of silver-mounted roller-skates of every size. If he encountered a maid at her work, he was likely to bid her put down her broom or duster and go skating.

There was another popular theory to account for the Duke's oddity, especially the manner of his visits to London. It was said that he had lived a double life, and, once arrived in the capital, became Mr T. C. Druce, a Baker Street upholsterer and a married man. This was widely believed, even though the said Druce had died in 1864 – it was whispered that his grave in Highgate cemetery contained only an empty coffin. As so much money was involved a lawsuit was started, but two branches of the Druce family fell out, and the attempt by one to get the grave opened was for many years blocked by the other. It was not until 30 December 1907, that the coffin was opened and found to contain the body of the upholsterer. So that legend was disposed of.

The mystery has not yet been explained and perhaps never will be. Probably the Duke, without being mad, was neurotic to an extraordinary degree, and being a wealthy aristocrat in that era was able to give his eccentricity full rein. Perhaps it had all begun after a certain episode which an eavesdropping servant, old Tinker, retailed in later years.

There had been one woman whom the future Duke, then the young Lord John, had loved and wished to marry: the famous actress, Fanny Kemble, whose portrait as Lady Macbeth was at Welbeck. Such a marriage was unthinkable. Tinker had heard the fourth Duke's horrified question, 'John, would you disgrace us?' and Lord John had stalked out of the room without another word. Soon afterwards, Fanny had gone to the United States and made an unhappy marriage with an American. Could the subsequent mystery of Welbeck have stemmed from Lord John's frustrated passion? At least no likelier explanation has yet appeared.

Carols in No Man's Land

'It will be over by Christmas.'

Everyone had said that confidently when Britain had gone to war with Germany on 4 August 1914. But now it was Christmas Eve, and there was no sign of an end to the slaughter.

At the start there had been a few exciting summer days with cavalry galloping across the countryside much as they had done in Napoleon's campaigns a century earlier. Then modern methods of warfare had taken over in all their horror. Machine-guns stopped the most heroic charge. High explosive shells blew men to pieces. Both sides had to dig themselves deep trenches for shelter and bolster them with sandbags. As autumn set in, they cowered there in the mud and water. The romance had gone out of war.

The two trench-systems, German and Allied, ran for hundreds of miles, from the North Sea to the Alps in neutral Switzerland. They formed elaborate zigzag patterns, with front lines and supporting lines and communicating trenches so that reinforcements and rations could come up from the rear. Only a narrow stretch of ground separated the two front lines: no man's land.

Every stealthy raid, every full-scale bayonet attack, had to come across that strip of shell-battered earth with its deep holes and stumps of trees. To raise one's head carelessly, to look over the parapet, was to ask for a sniper's bullet. It was safer to watch through a periscope. After dark, the sentries crouched in 'listening posts', straining their ears for the least noise of an approaching enemy.

On that first Christmas Eve of the Great War (which we now call the First World War) everyone hoped that the Germans would not attack. It was a home-sick time. Men's thoughts were with their families. It was a strange way to spend Christmas, shivering in a foreign trench, with murderous weapons laid ready for instant action. Six months ago, none of them would have believed it possible.

Suddenly – and at more than one place along the line – surprising sounds came floating from the German trenches opposite. The enemy – the 'hated Huns', the barbarous 'Boche' – were singing. And, though the words were in German, the tunes were familiar. They were carols.

Spontaneously the singing was taken up by some of the British. No one could say who began it and no one, even the fiercest sergeant-major, could stop it. The waves of song flowed across no man's land and blended in the middle.

And then, as if by some miracle – 'miracle' was the word used by a writer in *The Times* – not only was there 'singing upon one side answered by the other', but the soldiers began to clamber out of their trenches, no weapons in their hands but sometimes

holding out little gifts of chocolate or cigarettes. 'The men rose and advanced to meet each other as if they had been released from a spell . . . and some say that the darkness became strange and beautiful with lights as well as music, as if the armies had been gathered together not for war but for the Christmas feast.'

Does it sound like a sentimental story? It happened. The British commander, Field-Marshal Sir John French, wrote disapprovingly: 'When this was reported to me I issued immediate orders to prevent any recurrence of such conduct, and called the local commanders to strict account, which resulted in a good deal of trouble.'

It would never have done for the soldiers to make friends and think of each other as human beings. They must hate each other as monsters, or the war could not go on.

The generals put a stop to 'such conduct' and restored normal discipline. The war went on. It went on for nearly four years longer, during which two million Germans were killed, one million British Empire troops, and millions from the other nations involved.

The Field-Marshal, however, was not one of these. He lived on till 1925, when he was seventy-two, and had been made the Earl of Ypres for his military achievements. Ypres, from which he took his title, was the Belgian town which was the scene of three bitter battles during the war. In the first alone (where he commanded the British armies) their casualties totalled 54,106, killed, wounded or missing.

Christmas Banned

There are always a few people to grumble about the expense and upset involved in Christmas but it is hard today to imagine Parliament voting to abolish it.

Yet that is exactly what happened in 1652 when, following their victory in the Civil War, the Puritans held power in England.

On 24 December in that year, after a long debate on naval matters, the House of Commons 'were presented with a terrible Remonstrance against Christmas-day, grounded upon divine Scriptures: 2 Corinthians v. 16; 1 Corinthians xv. 14, 17', and arguing that it was only 'Mass-mongers' and 'Papists' who observed it.

There was an earnest discussion. The sombre-dressed, grave-faced Members sat there in their tall plain hats, rising in turn to bandy Bible texts and theological arguments. Then the House decided on 'the Abolition of Christmas-day, passed Orders to that Effect, and resolved to sit on the following Day, which was commonly called Christmas-day'. So runs the printed record in the *Flying Eagle Gazette*.

It was just another blow in the war against pleasure. In those years of Puritan rule the theatres were closed, the maypoles came down, football was forbidden, race-meetings banned, and even the churches deprived of their choirs and organs. Not all the supporters of Parliament were such kill-joys, but for a time the extremer Puritans had the bit between their teeth, and if a more moderate man like Oliver Cromwell wished to stay in the saddle he dared not speak out too boldly against them.

Disobedience could be dangerous. Evelyn's *Diary* tells what happened to that inoffensive gentleman on 25 December 1657.

He and his wife, good Church of England folk, still privately thinking of it as Christmas Day, went to morning service. After the sermon, the minister went on to the Holy Communion and the congregation filed up to kneel before the altar and receive the sacrament of bread and wine.

At that point the door was flung open and a party of musketeers clattered in, their weapons at the ready. The minister continued with the service, the worshippers knelt in turn, though some of the soldiers levelled their muskets at them from point-blank range. They seemed a little nonplussed, however, 'as perhaps not having instructions what to do in case they found us in that action', Evelyn recorded.

The soldiers allowed the service to be finished without interference. Then they arrested everyone who had taken part. Some were marched off, but the more notable prisoners, such as the Countess of Dorset, Lady Hatton, and the Evelyns, were treated with more respect. They were allowed to dine and then kept in a room under supervision until a Colonel Whaly and other officers arrived from Whitehall to interrogate them.

Evelyn tells how, when his turn came, they took his name and address and demanded to know how he dared to 'be at Common Prayers, which they told me was but the Mass in English'. They accused him of praying for Charles Stuart (the exile who returned three years later as Charles II) but he retorted that he had merely been praying for all Christian kings, princes and governors.

After some more 'frivolous and ensnaring questions and much threatening . . . finding no colour to detain me, they dismissed me with much pity of my ignorance', and Evelyn went thankfully home.

By 1660 it was all over. The Puritans were out, the Cavaliers were in. The maypoles went up again, the theatres opened, the choristers blossomed out in their white surplices and carolled out their anthems – and Christmas was merry again.

Yet things were never quite the same. The Puritans had left their mark on English life and the English character. The roistering spirit of Elizabethan and medieval times was never fully recaptured.

It would be pleasant to record that the churchgoers who had faced persecution by the Puritans now made sure that in future all Englishmen should be free to worship as they pleased. Unfortunately, the Restoration merely turned the tables. The Church of England was now on top again, and for the next century or two it saw that it stayed there, treating men with other beliefs, from Roman Catholics to Quakers, as second-class citizens.